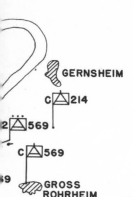

GERNSHEIM

C △ 214

2 △ 569

C △ 569

9

GROSS ROHRHEIM

BIBLIS

ADT

E

MAJ. GEN. J.W. O'DANIEL
COMMANDING 3d I

LT. GEN. W.H. HAISLIP
COMMANDING

AA OFFICER
COL. J.B. FRASER

NARRATIVE

ON THE 23 MARCH 1945, LEADING ELEMENTS OF THE XV CORPS, WHICH HAD THE MISSION OF ESTABLISHING A BRIDGEHEAD ACROSS THE RHINE, HAD REACHED THE WEST BANK OF THE RIVER. ANTIAIRCRAFT UNITS ATTACHED TO THE XV CORPS AND FURTHER ATTACHED TO THE 23d AAA GROUP WERE AS FOLLOWS: 34th AAA GROUP; 798th AAA AW BN (M), PROTECTING CORPS ARTILLERY; 838th AAA AW BN (M), PROTECTING SUPPLY INSTALLATIONS, L OF C's AND ENGINEER EQUIPMENT FOR THE RHINE RIVER CROSSING; 214th AAA GUN BN (M), PROTECTING FORWARD ZONE AND MSR; 777th AAA AW BN (SP), PROTECTING THE 6th ARMD DIV; 106th AAA AW BN (SP), PROTECTING THE 45th INF DIV; 441st AAA AW BN (SP), PROTECTING THE 3d INF DIV; 436th AAA AW BN (M), PROTECTING THE 63d INF DIV; BTRY A, 353d AA SLT BN PROVIDING "BATTLEFIELD ILLUMINATION" FOR THE 45th AND 3d INF DIV'S.

24th MARCH: THE ENGR COMBAT GROUPS (THE 540th AND 40th) THAT HAD THE MISSION OF CONSTRUCTING THE BRIDGES FOR THE RHINE CROSSING, HAVING ARRIVED IN FORWARD ASSEMBLY AREAS. THE 838th AAA AW BN (M) WAS RELIEVED OF ITS OTHER MISSIONS AND GIVEN THE MISSION OF PROTECTING THE 540th ENGR COMBAT GROUP WITH THE ENTIRE BATTALION. THE 569th AAA AW BN (M), UPON BEING ATTACHED TO THE CORPS, WAS GIVEN THE MISSION OF PROTECTING THE 40th ENGR COMBAT GROUP. THE 62d AAA GUN BN (M) UPON BEING ATTACHED TO THE CORPS WAS GIVEN THE MISSION OF FURNISHING GUN PROTECTION FOR THE R(S) HALF OF THE CORPS SECTOR, WITH THREE BATTERIES ON A GENERAL FORWARD LINE ABOUT FOUR THOUSAND YARDS FROM THE WEST BANK OF THE RIVER AND ONE BATTERY CENTRALLY LOCATED ABOUT SIX THOUSAND YARDS TO THE REAR; ALL BATTERIES TO GO INTO POSITION UNDER COVER OF DARKNESS. THE 214th AAA GUN BN WAS GIVEN A SIMILAR MISSION PROTECTING THE L(N) HALF OF THE CORPS SECTOR, ALL BATTERIES TO MOVE INTO POSITION UNDER COVER OF DARKNESS. THE 777th AAA AW BN (SP) PASSED FROM CORPS CONTROL ALONG WITH THE 6th ARMD DIV. OTHER UNITS NO CHANGE.

25th MARCH: THE 910th AAA AW BN (LESS I BATTERY) UPON BEING ATTACHED TO CORPS WAS GIVEN THE MISSION OF SUPPLEMENTING THE PROTECTION OF CORPS ARTILLERY IN FORWARD ASSEMBLY AREAS. THE 838th AAA AW BN (M) WAS MISSION OF PROTECTING THE 540th ENGR COMBAT GROUP WITH ONE BATTERY, REMAINING BATTERIES ON L OF C's AND CLASS III SUPPLY DUMPS. THE 44th DIV ARTILLERY BEING USED IN SUPPORT OF THE ATTACK, ELEMENTS OF THE 995th AAA AW BN (M) WERE MOVED FORWARD TO GIVE IT PROTECTION. THE REMAINDER OF THE 353d AA SLT BN UPON BEING ATTACHED TO THE CORPS WAS GIVEN THE MISSION OF FURNISHING GROUND ILLUMINATION FOR FRONT LINE UNITS ON CALL. NO CHANGE IN OTHER UNITS.

26th MARCH: AT 0230 (H HOUR) THE CROSSING WAS BEGUN, WITH TWO DIVISIONS ABREAST, THE 3d DIV ON THE RIGHT AND THE 45th DIV ON THE LEFT. THE 441st AAA AW BN (SP) AND THE 106th AAA AW BN (SP) CROSSED WITH THE DIVISIONS; CERTAIN UNITS BEING MOVED UP TO THE WEST BANK OF THE RIVER, AND ELEMENTS FERRIED TO THE EAST BANK, EARLY IN THE OPERATION, FURNISHING AUTOMATIC WEAPONS PROTECTION FROM THE EAST BANK AT STAGES OF THE CROSSING. THE 838th AND 569th AAA AW BNS MOVED FORWARD, PRIOR TO DAYBREAK, WITH THE ENGINEER GROUPS THEY WERE PROTECTING. INITIALLY THESE UNITS FURNISHED PROTECTION FROM THE WEST BANK OF THE RIVER, BUT IMMEDIATELY UPON COMPLETION OF THE FIRST BRIDGE, EACH BATTALION SENT ONE BATTERY TO THE EAST BANK OF THE RIVER. DURING THE DAY BOTH GUN BNS DISPLACED TWO BATTERIES FORWARD TO THE WEST BANK OF THE RIVER IN THE VICINITY OF THE BRIDGE SITES. ALL AW UNITS WITH CORPS ARTILLERY, DISPLACED TO POSITIONS NEARER THE WEST BANK OF THE RIVER. ANTICIPATING ATTACKS FROM THE DIRECTION OF THE SUN, TWO EXTRA RADAR SETS WERE SECURED AND UNDER COVER OF DARKNESS MOVED TO VIC OF THE TWO HEAVY PONTON BRIDGE SITES TO GIVE EARLY WARNING TO THE AW UNITS. THE 353d AA SLT BN MOVED CERTAIN LIGHTS TO THE WEST BANK OF THE RIVER, READY TO ILLUMINATE FLOATING DEBRIS, SWIMMERS, OR ANY OTHER OBJECTS SENT AGAINST THE BRIDGES BY THE ENEMY. THE 436th AAA AW BN (M) PASSED FROM CORPS CONTROL WITH 63d INF DIV. THE 572d AAA AW BN (SP) CAME UNDER CONTROL OF GROUP UPON ATTACHMENT OF THE 12th ARMD DIV TO THE CORPS.

27th MARCH: THE 838th AAA AW BN (M) AND THE 569th AAA AW BN (M) EACH COMPLETED THE MOVEMENT OF TWO BATTERIES ACROSS THE RIVER; THE 214th AAA GUN BN MOVED ONE BATTERY TO THE EAST BANK OF THE RIVER, AND DISPLACED ANOTHER BATTERY NEARER TO THE WEST BANK; THE 62d AAA GUN BN MOVED ONE BATTERY ACROSS EARLY IN THE MORNING, AND ANOTHER BATTERY ACROSS DURING THE NIGHT. ELEMENTS OF AW UNITS WITH CORPS ARTILLERY AND WITH ATTACHED DIVISIONS CROSSED DURING THE PERIOD.

28th MARCH: THE 214th AAA GUN BN (M) COMPLETED ITS FINAL DISPOSITIONS WITH THE MOVEMENT OF A SECOND BATTERY ACROSS THE RIVER AND THE BATTERIES ON THE WEST SIDE INTO THEIR FINAL POSITIONS; THE 62d AAA GUN BN MOVED ITS BATTERIES ON THE WEST SIDE INTO THEIR FINAL POSITIONS.

THE ENEMY MADE REPEATED AIR ATTACKS FOR SEVERAL DAYS PRIOR TO THE CROSSING, AS WELL AS DURING THE OPERATION, WITH THE ANTIAIRCRAFT BRINGING DOWN A GOOD PERCENTAGE OF THE ATTACKING PLANES. THE HIGHLIGHT OF THE OPERATION WAS THE DEFINITE DESTRUCTION OF SEVEN OF THE TWELVE PLANES ATTACKING ON THE NIGHT OF 25-26 MARCH, THE NIGHT THE CROSSING BEGAN, AND THE PROBABLE DESTRUCTION OF THREE OTHERS. NO DAMAGE WAS DONE TO ANY OF THE BRIDGES, OR OTHER INSTALLATIONS, AND THE CROSSING OF THE CORPS WAS UNINTERRUPTED. THREE INFANTRY DIVISIONS, ONE ARMORED DIVISION AND ALL CORPS TROOPS CROSSED IN RECORD TIME, ESTABLISHING A BRIDGEHEAD FOR THE SEVENTH ARMY.

△

MAJ. GEN. W.F. DEAN
COMMANDING

ANTIAIRCRAFT DISPOSITIONS
RHINE RIVER CROSSING OF XV CORPS
SEVENTH UNITED STATES ARMY
26TH MARCH TO 28TH MARCH 1945
SCALE=1:60,000 APPROX.

YARDS 1000 500 0   1000   2,000   3000

MILES 1   0   1

SUBMITTED A. E. Dunstan APPROVED Douglas Iver Ruff
MAJ., 23d AAA GP   LT. COL., 23d AAA GP

The General

WILLIAM LEVINE,
CITIZEN SOLDIER AND LIBERATOR

The General

WILLIAM LEVINE,
CITIZEN SOLDIER AND LIBERATOR

By **ALEX KERSHAW** and **RICHARD ERNSBERGER, JR.**

Introduction by Colonel (IL) Jennifer N. Pritzker, IL ARNG (Retired)

PRITZKER
MILITARY
MUSEUM & LIBRARY

2016

Library of Congress Cataloging-in-Publication Data
Title: *The General: William Levine, Citizen Soldier and Liberator* by Alex Kershaw and Richard Ernsberger, Jr., with an introduction by Colonel (IL) Jennifer N. Pritzker, IL ARNG (Retired)
Description: 128 pages: illustrated with black and white photographs; cm.
Includes bibliographical references and index.
Identifiers: ISBN 978-0-9897928-8-2 (hardcover) | ISBN 978-0-9897928-9-9 (e-book)
Subjects: LCSH: 1. World War, 1939-1945. 2. Cold War. 3. Dachau (concentration camp). 4. Illinois – Fort Sheridan. 5. United States – Army – Officers –Biography. 6. Jewish soldiers – United States – Biography. 7. Holocaust, Jewish (1939-1945). 8. Levine, William P., 1915-2013.
Names: Kershaw, Alex, author. | Ernsberger, Richard, author. | Pritzker, Jennifer N., contributor.
Classification: LCC E840.5.L46 K47 2016 | DDC 355

Executive Editors:
Colonel (IL) Jennifer N. Pritzker, IL ARNG (Retired)
Kenneth Clarke
Designer: Wendy Palitz

Photographs and documents courtesy of the Pritzker Military Museum & Library, except for the following: page 45, U.S. Army/National Archives; page 49, top: T4 Arland B. Musser/U.S. Army/National Archives; page 49, bottom: PFC Dennis/U.S. Army/National Archives; page 50, bottom: Joboul Publishing Co.; page 51, top: courtesy of John Levine; page 51, bottom: Oscar Sotelo/U.S. Army/National Archives; page 55, bottom: courtesy of Rhoda Levine; page 58, photograph by Mark D. Wasserman.

To access the Major General William P. Levine Archive at the Pritzker Military Museum & Library search www.pritzkermilitary.org with William P. Levine in the search parameters or contact the Museum & Library to request an appointment.

The trade edition of *The General: William Levine, Citizen Soldier and Liberator*, was preceded by a limited edition of 100 numbered copies with a unique tip-in page.

First Edition

CONTENTS

Introduction

To those who knew him, Major General William P. Levine, USAR (Retired), was a family man, a businessman and a devoted man of faith. He was also known as a military man whose long years of service to his country were eclipsed by his experience as a U.S. Army Soldier who helped liberate the Dachau concentration camp during World War II.

Bill Wambsgnass, the Cleveland Indians second baseman who performed the only unassisted triple play in baseball history during the 1920 World Series, once said about his triple play "you would think I was born the day before and died the day after." Such was eventually the case with William Levine: Late in his life, when people asked about his military experience, they only wanted to know about Dachau, and Dachau is what he talked about.

The Pritzker Military Museum & Library wanted to know more. We wanted to know why a man who was drafted into the U.S. Army in 1942 as a private decided to stay in the military after World War II—Levine retired as a Major General in 1975—the highest rank obtainable for a U.S. Army Reserve soldier at the time. We wanted to know about the man who in his 70s suddenly decided to talk about his WWII experiences after decades of silence. And we wanted to know about the family man who devoted many of his retirement years volunteering at several synagogues near his home in Chicago's northern suburbs.

Our curiosity was sparked by Levine and his family who generously donated his entire collection of books, correspondence, maps, uniforms, photos, field manuals, and medals to the PMML. The collection contains three pistols, including his general officer Colt .32 caliber sidearm that is on loan at the Illinois Holocaust Museum and Education Center, and a Walther PP 7.65 mm taken from a German officer and brought home with the permission of the Headquarters United States Forces European Theater (see page 47).

Levine passed away in March of 2013 at the age of 97 just as the Museum & Library began working on this book. His wife Rhoda, son John, and other family members, close friends, and staff of the Museum & Library gave generously to help add essential depth and life to Levine's archive at the Museum & Library and to help preserve a legacy for Levine that he would have wanted.

Levine was the quintessential citizen soldier. He was a man who in his youth had no desire for anything military, but when his country called, he as a loyal citizen gave without hesitation.

As a Jew he was profoundly shocked by the Nazi genocide of 6 million Jews, and millions of others, individuals who were killed simply for being who they were. His experiences convinced him that in order for the United States to remain free and avoid the atrocities he witnessed during WWII, the United States needed a strong, well-equipped, well-trained, well-led military at all times.

Following the war, he became a multicareer citizen soldier. This story of his life will show readers the complexity of simultaneous integration of a military career, business career, philanthropic career, and active family life. Levine was successful at all of these things.

The PMML is a living monument to people like Major General Levine. It is a place where citizens and soldiers meet, study, and discuss and analyze military affairs and history so that all can learn from the past to better understand the present and gather ideas to shape the future. One of the lessons that Levine helps teach is that if the United States military is needed to protect our liberty and freedom, it cannot function without the support of a ready Reserves and the National Guard, whether it be mobilized and deployed or performing endless tasks essential to train people and maintain equipment for the moment of need.

We owe a debt of gratitude for the decades of service provided by William Levine, and the best way to repay that debt is to learn from his life of distinguished service.

—Colonel (IL) Jennifer N. Pritzker, IL ARNG (Retired)

PART ONE

The War Years
From Normandy to Dachau

BY ALEX KERSHAW

The world seemed to have been drained of color. The bloodiest conflict in human history would be over in a matter of days. A young captain with the Seventh Army's intelligence staff, weary of war and anxious to get home to his wife, neared a small town north of Munich, the birthplace of Nazism. In the far distance loomed the jagged peaks of the Tyrol, snowcapped and forbidding. The town the American captain entered was called Dachau—a neat little burg with well-tended gardens, stolidly bourgeois, deserted.

Never would the American captain forget what he would see that day, April 29, 1945, amid gray barracks on the outskirts of the charming Bavarian town. The images, which would be seared forever into his mind, defied human reason in their cruelty, suffering, and pain. They would prove an enormous burden, casting a long and secret shadow over much of the rest of the captain's long life. No matter how hard he would try to come to terms with the experience, April 29, 1945, would leave him forever scarred. Something deep inside would be damaged. Only forty years later would he be able to start to talk about what had happened in Dachau the day it was liberated. Then it would be impossible to hold back the tears and sobs.

AS WITH SO MANY of those of his generation who rose rapidly through the ranks of the U.S. military in WWII, William P. Levine had been born into modest circumstances—in his case, in July 1915, the year that Babe Ruth hit his first major league home run and the ocean liner *Lusitania* was sunk in the Atlantic. The son of a hard-working Russian immigrant father, he had grown up in Minnesota on the shores of Lake Superior, always aware that the U.S. was a sanctuary for Jews taking refuge from persecution in Europe. His father had escaped pogroms in tsarist Russia, emigrating from the town of Ekaterinoslav on the banks of the Dnieper River in the Ukraine, arriving in Minnesota via Liverpool and Canada in June 1910 at age twenty-two.[1]

According to a relative, Levine senior had "a talent for happiness, a rare and precious talent, which he shared with all his loved ones and friends."[2] Levine's mother Sadie, who helped his father run a small grocery store, lived by the adage, "If you don't have something nice to say don't say anything at all." She was strict with Levine and his three younger brothers, especially when it came to eating healthily and getting exercise. When they showed an interest in smoking, she began to smoke a cigarette in front of them, almost choking and starting to cry. Her sons quickly got the message.[3] Sadie Levine would live to the age of 103, dying in 1998.

Levine was also very much a son of Duluth, located at the westernmost point of the Great Lakes on the north shore of Lake Superior, the largest freshwater lake in the world. Although Duluth was a city of some 100,000, Levine remembered it having the feel of a small town. In his eyes, Duluth didn't have the "cliques and animosities that you might find in a large, metropolitan area."[4] Indeed, the city was a joyous place to grow up for Levine, who played a lot of hockey and basketball in the winter and baseball in the summer. It was a city of rattling streetcars that connected the waterfront to inland hills, described by some as "The San Francisco of the Midwest."

Levine was athletic and studious. He attended Duluth Central High School and then the University of Minnesota, where he majored in zoology and psychology.[5] He excelled academically, but only a few months shy of receiving his degree he left college to find work to support himself. Jobs were hard to come by in Duluth during the Depression, yet he managed to find a sales position at the Paramount Garment Company, which produced made-to-measure men's clothing.[6] In 1941, he married a supportive young woman called Leah, and the future looked bright for twenty-six-year-old Levine. But then came the bombing of Pearl Harbor on December 7, 1941, "the day that would live in infamy" as President Roosevelt famously put it, followed three days later by Hitler's declaration of war on the United States.[7] America rapidly mobilized for war on two fronts, against formidable foes in Europe and the Pacific. Along with millions of his generation, Levine was drafted into the army, in his case in 1942. His enlistment record described him as a married clothing salesman, with dark brown hair, hazel eyes, weighing 150 pounds and measuring five feet, nine inches.[8]

Levine would later stress that he felt a very strong sense of "responsibility" to his wife Leah. He had been in no hurry to enlist because that would have meant leaving her alone.[9] So he had decided to await the draft, hoping he might gain extra months at her side. He would also later joke that he was a "devout coward," far from eager to become a soldier, certainly not one to rush toward the sound of the guns.[10] Yet Levine quickly took to army life, so much so that during his basic training as a private in Texas, he decided to become a commissioned officer. This would give him, he believed, "a greater degree of latitude in his movement and performance." As an officer, he "might be of a greater value not only to [himself] but to the Army."[11]

In the summer of 1943, Levine completed officer training, receiving the highest possible marks. He was then placed in charge of a company of engineers for a short time before being assigned to the artillery to work in intelligence with the Thirty-fourth Anti-Aircraft Artillery (AAA) Group.[12] Levine's wife, Leah, accompanied him as he trained at various bases in the American

HE WOULD ALSO LATER JOKE THAT HE WAS A "DEVOUT COWARD," FAR FROM EAGER TO BECOME A SOLDIER

South before being posted overseas. In Leah's diaries from this period, there are clues to the often lonely and depressing lives of military wives in wartime America, references to roach-infested married quarters, "Mexican heartburn" in El Paso, and often "lonesome" evenings, some spent in tears, as she shuffled from one drab military base to another.[13]

Evidently Second Lieutenant William Levine had the makings of a first-class intelligence officer: on February 5, 1944, while based in Louisiana, he was commended by the commanding officer of the Thirty-fourth AAA for "outstanding" performance in a combat intelligence test.[14] A month later, Levine departed the U.S., bound for Europe, having qualified as a marksman with an M-1 rifle.[15] Levine's chief role in combat would be reconnaissance. He would have to assess quickly and accurately what lay ahead of his unit, reporting on all potential obstacles and challenges, providing critical information that would enable senior officers to make the most effective decisions.[16]

Levine arrived in England in the early spring of 1944. For several weeks he joined the Allied forces responsible for defending the coastline along the English Channel. By May 1944, the whole area had become the largest supply depot in history, filled with tens of thousands of vehicles, weapons, and other vast stores in preparation for the greatest amphibious invasion in history, Operation Overlord. At some point, Levine learned that he would depart from Plymouth and arrive in Fortress Europe on D Day with fellow officers from the Thirty-fourth AAA, who would be assigned to the Fourth Division. They would land on a beach called Utah, the code name for the most westerly of the five landing sectors in Normandy.

As an intelligence officer, Levine would have known that the U.S. Fourth Infantry Division, aided by the Seventieth Tank Battalion, would storm Utah several hours after critical landings by paratroops. Indeed, in the first minutes of D Day, the 101st and Eighty-second Airborne Divisions would drop into the darkness of Nazi-occupied France to secure exits from Utah leading to the nearby town of Sainte-Mère-Église. These airborne troops, with barely any armored support, would also seize Sainte-Mère-Église itself to prevent the Germans from reinforcing Cherbourg, at the northern point of the Cotentin peninsula. The Allied invasion plans, which General Bernard Montgomery had amended to include Utah, called for the capture of the channel port as soon as possible to allow resupply of men and material.

Securing a beachhead in Normandy would be the Allies' greatest challenge of the war so far. Victory in Europe depended on it. On D Day, June 6, 1944, Levine crossed the channel in the early hours with the Fourth Division, part of the VII Corps commanded by Major General J. Lawton Collins, who had crucial prior experience with amphibious invasions in the Pacific. Levine was one of over 130,000 Allied troops that day who, before landing, heard the address of Allied Supreme Commander, Dwight D. Eisenhower—words that would define Levine and his generation's greatest mission: "The eyes of the world are upon you. The hopes and prayers of liberty-loving people everywhere march with you. In company with our brave Allies and brothers-in-arms on other Fronts, you will bring about the destruction of the German war machine, the elimination of Nazi tyranny over the oppressed peoples of Europe, and security for ourselves in a free world."[17]

Levine was fortunate indeed to have been selected to join the Fourth Division—the "Ivy" Division suffered just 197 casualties as it landed on D Day, an astonishingly low number given that 21,000 men came ashore that day on Utah.[18] The numbers killed and wounded were, notably, far less than on "Bloody Omaha," where the Americans suffered around 2,000 casualties. Omaha's formidable beach defenses had not been destroyed by Allied bombing, unlike on Utah, which had been accurately and heavily hit by some 300 B-26 Marauders that morning.[19] The Utah landings in fact proved to be the least costly and most successful on D Day. Within two hours of dropping into the area, the Eighty-second Airborne had seized crossroads at Sainte-Mère-Église. The Fourth Infantry Division, whose assistant division commander was Brigadier General Theodore Roosevelt, Jr., the oldest man to land on D Day, pushed quickly inland, soon linking up with airborne troops.

It was, fittingly, on the first day of Eisenhower's "Great Crusade" that William Levine got his first taste of what he later called "the horror of war."[20] As Levine came ashore on Utah, he later recalled, he spotted the corpse of a GI who had been decapitated, one of the comparatively few fatalities on Utah, most of which were caused by mines. Levine looked at death for the first time and found it, in his words, "rather disconcerting" and "quite disturbing."[21] He would also later remember it as "a harrowing experience."[22] He quickly pushed the image of the dead American to the back of his mind so he could function at his best.[23]

The Fourth Division moved further inland, initially meeting little resistance. Levine soon spotted a road sign. "It was a porcelain-covered sign," he recalled, "[with] a white border with blue field and with white lettering and the words Ste. Mere Eglise." He had been used to seeing words daubed on a piece of metal back in Minnesota. For the rest of his life, he would remember the fragile beauty of the porcelain sign, marking the first town in Europe he entered as a liberator.[24]

By the second week of June, the fighting in Normandy was growing ever more bloody as the Germans launched fierce counterattacks. It would sometimes take an infantry company an entire day to seize just one heavily defended field in the ancient maze of thick hedgerows and pastures known as the *bocage*. Cherbourg was liberated on June 25, but the port itself had been put out of action when the Germans had sunk ships and blown up key parts of the harbor. The Ivy Division had by then paid a mighty price, suffering over 5,000 casualties with over 800 men killed.[25]

The Germans proved to be masters of defensive warfare, fighting stubbornly even when the situation seemed hopeless, inflicting maximum casualties. On June 30, the celebrated war correspondent Ernie Pyle, who had accompanied the Fourth

Division for over two weeks, wrote to a friend, "This hedge to hedge stuff is a type of warfare we've never run into before, and I've seen more dead Germans than ever in my life. Americans too, but not nearly so many as the Germans. One day I'll think I'm getting hardened to dead people, dead young people in vast numbers, and then next day I'll realize I'm not and never could

"I'D REACHED A POINT WHERE I FELT THAT NO IDEAL WAS WORTH THE DEATH OF ONE MORE MAN."

be."[26] Pyle had seen "too much death" wherever he turned. "I'd become so revolted, so nauseated by the sight of swell kids having their heads blown off," Pyle later told a fellow reporter, "I'd lost track of the whole point of the war. I'd reached a point where I felt that no ideal was worth the death of one more man."[27]

Levine never lost track of the point of the war. He loathed Nazism and was, of course, a Jew. But at this stage he had no idea of the enormity of the Holocaust, then entering its most fatal chapter with the deportation to Auschwitz of Hungary's Jews. Over 400,000 Hungarian Jews were in fact murdered that summer, one every two seconds.[28] Countless communities throughout Europe had been liquidated. In Levine's father's home city of Ekaterinoslav in the Ukraine, over 30,000 Jews had been slaughtered.[29] Although Levine worked in army intelligence, he heard nothing that June and July in Normandy about this genocide or the concentration camps, where over a million Europeans were incarcerated, and the fast deteriorating conditions within them. It was later in August, as the Allies broke out of Normandy, having suffered over 400,000 casualties, that Levine began to receive "snippets" of information about the terrible conditions, but nothing detailed.[30]

French and American troops, some of whom had landed on Utah beside Levine, liberated Paris on August 25, 1944—"the day the war should have ended," according to the American writer Irwin Shaw who was in the French capital celebrating with delirious crowds.[31] It had been hoped that Berlin would soon follow. Eisenhower had been among the optimists, betting the war would be over by Christmas.[32] More than ever Hitler's victims depended for survival on the speed of advance of the Allies, but that fall it ground to a halt in some sectors. Spurred by Nazi propaganda and genuine patriotism, many German soldiers fought with a newfound ferocity now that the Fatherland was in peril. They had not fought for over four years to suddenly lay down their weapons when the enemy reached their borders.[33]

Debate raged among senior Allied generals about how best to end the war. The increasingly bitter argument was won by Eisenhower, who insisted on proceeding along a broad front, as opposed to Montgomery and Patton, who argued that a single powerful thrust to the heart of industrial Germany, through the Ruhr, would shorten the conflict, thereby saving lives. After the failure of Operation Market Garden that September—Montgomery's ambitious plan to cross the Rhine in Holland with airborne troops—the Allies found themselves stalled along Germany's western borders and bogged down in bloody and enervating fighting in the Huertgen Forest, where eleven U.S. divisions would receive a terrible and arguably fruitless mauling.

Then came Hitler's last gamble, his surprise counterattack in the Ardennes on December 16, 1944, that became known as the Battle of the Bulge, the largest land battle ever fought by the United States Army, involving over 600,000 men. It was indeed Hitler's final roll of the dice in the west, deeply flawed in conception and practice, and by mid-January of 1945, in bitter winter conditions, U.S. forces had pushed the Germans back to where they had launched their last great strike against American forces.

The great challenge that faced the Allies early in 1945 was how to cross the last natural barrier separating them from Berlin—the mighty Rhine, which had defeated Montgomery the previous fall. When the snow began to melt, the Allies pursued the broad front strategy, striking toward the heart of the Third Reich from Holland to Italy. The first Americans to cross the Rhine, soldiers of the Ninth Armored Division, did so at Remagen on March 9, capturing the famed Ludendorff Bridge. Yet the Germans still fought ferociously, incurring heavy casualties even as the Third Reich entered its last days. In March alone, over 350,000 German soldiers would be killed in defense of the Fatherland. Hitler's hold on power was still unassailable, his fanatical followers legion, ordinary citizens prepared to endure to the bitter end, victims of propaganda, self-delusion, and the extraordinary apparatus of terror that the SS and Gestapo had zealously created under SS Reichsfuhrer Heinrich Himmler.[34]

By the time the Allies had established a bridgehead on the eastern banks of the Rhine, William P. Levine's Thirty-fourth AAA had been assigned to the Seventh Army, which included the Forty-second and Forty-fifth Infantry Divisions. As spring beckoned, Levine entered Germany. Far more information about the Nazis' vast gulag of concentration and labor camps began to "filter through" to Levine as the Seventh Army was fast approaching locations of the notorious camps.[35] Levine learned that the "health of the people in the camps was at a very low level."[36] It was clear to him that there would be a "great need for medical support and assistance."[37] He also discovered that trainloads of prisoners were being moved from one camp to another, ahead of the Soviet advance, in what was left of Nazi Germany.[38] The Red Army had liberated Auschwitz on January 27, finding unimaginable horrors but relatively few survivors: over 50,000 inmates had been sent west on death marches to camps such as Bergen-Belsen, Neuengamme, Ravensbrück, and Dachau, which were as a result now massively overcrowded with the last surviving victims of Nazi terror.

AS LEVINE MADE HIS WAY south toward Bavaria with the Seventh Army, less than a hundred miles to his east, a wiry and intense seventeen-year-old Jewish soldier with the Red Army, Leon Kotlowsky, approached the Elbe River. Kotlowsky had grown up in Warsaw when the city had been home to Europe's largest Jewish community. After the outbreak of the war in September 1939, he and his family had fled to the Soviet Union where he had joined the Red Army. By the time he neared the Elbe River that April of 1945, three-quarters of his native Poland's Jews had been killed, over 3 million in all, including many of Kotlowsky's relatives.[39]

Kotlowsky certainly had every reason to loathe the Nazis, and to take pride and delight in killing them. He had started out in

1942 in the Red Army by "polishing officers' boots."[40] Then he had joined a tank crew. As the casualty lists grew—over 8 million Soviet soldiers would die—he was rapidly promoted.[41] By the spring of 1945, he commanded a company of T-34 tanks. He was still just seventeen but already a highly experienced leader of men in combat. Before his sixteenth birthday, he had in fact fought at Stalingrad, the turning point of the war for Germany on the Eastern Front, in which Von Paulus's Sixth Army had been destroyed, with over 90,000 prisoners taken, among them twenty-two of Hitler's generals.

Since the fall of Stalingrad in February 1943, Kotlowsky had endured many other bitterly contested battles on the Eastern Front where the Wehrmacht had been bled almost dry, suffering three-quarters of its total WWII fatalities of well over 4 million. He had also learned of the horrors of the Holocaust, especially in the Ukraine, where some 800,000 Jews had been murdered during Nazi occupation.[42] He had in fact visited the ravine called Babi Yar, on the outskirts of Kiev, where the Nazis had shot tens of thousands of his fellow Jews.[43] Atrocity after atrocity had occurred there, the most infamous having taken place in September 1941 when over 33,000 Jews were killed in what was thought to be the largest single massacre in the history of the Holocaust to that date.[44]

On April 25, 1945, U.S. and Red Army forces linked up near Torgau, southwest of Berlin, and danced together, drunk on vodka, as comrades in arms. The following day, Kotlowsky also reached the Elbe. "When I came out of [my] tank I was unshaven and dirty," he recalled. "The village on the Russian side had been destroyed."[45] He spotted a boat, containing several American soldiers, as it crossed the river. Some of his fellow Red Army soldiers sent up a loud cheer. Then the Americans and Red Army men gathered together, the Americans shouldering their M-1s and pulling out bars of chocolate and packets of gum. "From somewhere, a bottle of vodka was produced and everyone toasted their mutual victory," Kotlowsky remembered.[46]

LEVINE AND KOTLOWSKY REPRESENTED
VERY DIFFERENT STATISTICAL FATES
FOR JEWS IN UNIFORM

To celebrate their meeting, and indeed the joining up of the Allied armies, the Americans and Soviets fired their guns in the air as a "salute to each other." "We were all very friendly and happy," recalled Kotlowsky. "We went to a house which was badly damaged and the Americans came and met [us]. We sat together round a table. We gave them vodka. The Americans gave us whisky and we exchanged cigarettes. They had Camel and Lucky Strike cigarettes.... The Americans could only speak English. We could speak only Russian and Polish."

How could they possibly communicate? Kotlowsky knew it was unlikely but perhaps one of the Americans spoke Yiddish?

"Ratzs du, Yiddish? [Do you speak Yiddish?]" he asked the Americans.

"Yah [Yes]," replied Captain William H. Levine.

Levine and Kotlowksy were soon chatting away, answering the questions of both groups of soldiers in a language that had been almost wiped out in just five years in Eastern Europe. The meeting was a highlight of the war for both men, providing never to be forgotten moments of genuine joy and comradeship. Neither could know that the Cold War, pitting Soviets against Americans, was about to start with a vengeance.[47] "We sat together for two and a half hours," recalled Kotlowsky, "all very friendly and happy. The American officers invited us to the West side that evening to go to a meeting. This didn't happen because the NKVD [The Communist Secret Police] came [and forbade it]. . . ."[48]

Levine and Kotlowksy represented very different statistical fates for Jews in uniform in WWII. Levine was one of around 550,000 Jewish Americans who served in WWII, of whom some 11,000 were killed.[49] Of the 500,000-odd Jews like Kotlowsky who fought with the Red Army, an astonishing 40% were fatalities.[50] Life expectancy in the Red Army had been short indeed.

For Leon Kotlowsky the war was over. He would soon return to the Soviet Union and see his father for the first time in five years. He would also discover that most of his Polish relatives had died in the Holocaust. For Captain William Levine, by contrast, the war raged on. He was by now a wily veteran, he later recalled, seemingly inured to the innumerable horrors of the conflict, or at least he thought he was: "We had all been in combat. We had seen death in very violent forms, and not that you become hardened to it, but you learn to live with it in a fashion. I guess your mind accommodates it so that the mission you are required to perform can be accomplished without interference."[51] Effective officers like Levine had to become somewhat numbed to the agonies of war or they risked psychological breakdown. Indeed, feelings had to be buried if Levine was to function at his best, finally get the job done after eleven months of combat, and hopefully get home in one piece to his anxious wife and family in Minnesota. He had only to survive a few more weeks.

AFTER THE MEETING on the Elbe, Levine rejoined the Seventh Army's advance. Munich was the next objective, the birthplace of Nazism, and further south still stood Hitler's mountain retreat at Berchtesgarden, the so-called Eagle's Nest where Allied intelligence had indicated that Hitler was preparing to make a last stand with his most fanatical SS followers. Levine was now receiving excellent and detailed information about the enemy, its strengths and weaknesses, as well as about horrific camps that had yet to be liberated.

Late that April of 1945, Levine's unit was rolling fast to the south, meeting scant resistance, through an apparently bucolic Bavaria that Levine would later describe as a "lovely part of the world." He had been attached to a group of intelligence officers who would accompany Seventh Army troops from the Forty-fifth and Forty-second Divisions, which had been assigned the task of liberating Hitler's first concentration camp, Dachau, some twelve miles north of Munich. As he approached Dachau, Levine had time to admire the famed Danube River. It was not a wonderful blue, rather a dirty gray, but he still found it impressive. He couldn't help but think of the "wonderful waltz," "Blue Danube," that he had heard so many times back in Duluth. The romantic music, which he loved, didn't seem to "fit with the reasons" why he was in Germany.[52]

At some point on April 29, 1945, Levine later recalled, he reached the outskirts of the town of Dachau. He knew that the

Dachau complex, which contained a Waffen SS barracks and training area as well as a concentration camp, stood on the edge of the town, literally in view of many homes. It was arguably the most notorious concentration camp in the Third Reich, certainly the longest standing. Since opening on March 22, 1933, just fifty-one days after Hitler took power, over 200,000 "undesirable elements"[53] had passed through the camp, and at least 30,000 had died there, over 13,000 in 1945 alone.[54] Some 32,000 inmates were still inside. For several months, many had waited ever more anxiously, hoping the SS would not massacre them in a final act of barbarism.

It was a cold, overcast day. Snow threatened as Levine entered the town. In some homes, white sheets were hanging from windows, signaling surrender. It was eerily quiet, as if the entire town was holding its breath in anticipation of the Americans' arrival. Dachau was as pretty as anywhere in Bavaria: cobbled streets skirted by timber-framed homes with brightly painted shutters. There were fresh beds of spring flowers.[55]

Levine came across some railroad tracks that led toward the southern perimeter of the sprawling Dachau complex. He then caught sight of the complex itself for the first time.[56] It resembled some kind of garrison, surrounded by a ten-foot brick wall.[57] Levine approached a train standing motionless on the rail line. He looked into a boxcar. It contained dead bodies. The corpses were just skin and bones. Human excrement was all around.[58] In another boxcar, decomposing corpses lay riddled with bullets from strafing, no doubt from Allied planes. The open boxcars were not marked with the POW sign to indicate they carried prisoners. The victims inside must have been terrified before they died.[59]

Levine was stunned as he looked into two more boxcars.[60] But he was still able to think straight, unlike others who had come across the same scenes and lost all composure, breaking down in tears and vomiting. Levine told a medic that the bodies needed to be moved as soon as possible because they were a health hazard. As he would later put it, "death should not be left unattended

AS HE WOULD LATER PUT IT, "DEATH SHOULD NOT BE LEFT UNATTENDED FOR LONG."

for long." Levine also recalled that the "stench was horrible—both of the human excrement and actual death."[61] It hung in the air, heavy, sweet, nauseating. It would cling to liberators' uniforms long after they had left the scene. It was clear to Levine that hundreds of people had died before the train had arrived in Dachau. Their suffering was beyond imagining. How could human beings possibly treat others this way?

Some men near Levine stood frozen in disbelief and stared at the corpse-strewn boxcars. Some of the dead had open eyes. Their last moments of agony were etched on their skeletal faces. It was as if others were staring at Levine's fellow liberators, remembered one man, and asking, "What took you so long?"[62] Many of the victims were naked. Some appeared to have been whipped savagely. One dead man lay on bodies having cut off his gangrenous leg with his own hands. The stump was covered in dirty paper.[63]

There were thirty-nine boxcars in all, containing some 2,000 corpses. The train had left Buchenwald with around 4,800 prisoners three weeks earlier. It had first stopped so that hundreds could be shot.[64] On April 21, when the train halted for the second time, 3,100 severely malnourished and dehydrated people had still been alive.[65] Six days later, when it had pulled into Dachau at night, there had been just 800.[66] The dead had been left to rot on the abandoned train.[67]

Levine moved on, past the death train, and entered the Dachau complex[68] where he spotted a group of survivors. Levine was "almost overpowered" by the desire to do something for them.[69] Levine moved closer: many were in striped uniforms, so very close to death, so emaciated they could barely stand. He suddenly realized they were all at different "stages of dying" in so many agonizing ways, from exhaustion, malnutrition, and disease.[70] Wherever he now looked, he saw men near the end, some in the final minutes of life. One man lay on the ground in his inmate's uniform with his eyes wide open, breathing his last.[71]

Levine would later recall feeling many different emotions that day: rage, crushing sadness, pity, and, above all, compassion. He was not, after almost a year in combat, utterly numb, brutalized beyond feeling.[72] The impulse to help the inmates was indeed overwhelming. Some GIs handed over cigarettes and boxes of K rations. Others held back. They had been ordered not to hand over any food because it might be too much for the severely malnourished. Some of the men alongside Levine were Jewish. They knew that many people in the camp were also Jewish. Levine later remembered that his fellow Jewish soldiers "probably felt that if they looked at me they might get a clue as to what they should be feeling or exhibiting, much the same as if [they were at a movie and somebody was laughing]:

We were all rather bug-eyed at what we were looking at. It was almost in disbelief that we saw this horror. One young fellow actually began to sob, an Italian kid. He cried softly. Another fellow looked almost as if he wasn't seeing anything. His eyes weren't even focused on anything. And as far as I was concerned, I could almost identify with some of the inmates because I was Jewish . . . [73]

It was a question that many other liberators asked: What could these people have done to deserve this kind of hell? Levine also reflected momentarily on how long they must have been there. Realizing how greatly they must have suffered "boggled [his] mind."[74] Levine would also later recall,

There was no way we could have been prepared for the utter horror of what we saw. The first sight of the boxcars on railroad tracks leading into the camp, with many dead bodies strewn on the floor and some bodies left alongside the tracks where they had fallen, did not prepare us for the sickening sight and stench inside the camp. The view of hundreds of men and women in dirty and tattered prison uniforms, all with sunken-hollow faces, staring, unblinking eyes, fleshless limbs, torsos with sallow skin tightly outlining their skeletal frames filled us with revulsion and anger. We all had been through a long period of combat with soldiers killing and maiming the enemy, but this was [a case of] armed soldiers, killing and mistreating defenseless civilians, purposely.[75]

LEVINE WALKED FURTHER INTO the Dachau concentration camp. He had yet to enter any of the drab gray buildings. He

approached a young man, a Belgian called Maurice Pioro,[76] who was about to collapse. Levine grabbed him, preventing him from falling, held him in his arms, then carried him into a nearby barrack. It was surprisingly easy to carry the man—he didn't weigh much, thanks to prolonged malnutrition.[77] "I felt that he had to be in some kind of enclosure instead of out in the yard there," recalled Levine, who placed the man on a cot. He then looked around and saw how primitive conditions were. The bunks were just knocked together, row upon row of flimsy deathbeds, holding men at the end of their endurance and the silent dead.

"My God," thought Levine, "how can these people sleep and rest on these hard wood boards when their bodies have no meat, just skin and bone?"

Levine looked around. Some of the inmates were so close to death they were unable even to celebrate their liberation.[78] He left the barrack, exiting into the foul-smelling air, and continued through the camp.[79] The stench of death reminded some men of the smell of a stockyard. The young man whom Levine had helped was one of 31,432 people still alive inside KZ Dachau on April 29, 1945. The largest contingents of survivors were Polish (9,082) and Russian (4,258). There were also over a thousand Catholic priests and 2,539 Jews.[80]

Levine continued through the camp, past the confinement area where the daily roll calls were held. It was surrounded by a high barbed-wire fence, which was skirted on one side by a canal. Sections of the fence were still electrified. To touch it meant certain death.[81] Levine knew that elements of the Forty-fifth and Forty-second Divisions had secured the camp earlier that day. The first liberators had in fact belonged to I Company of the 157th

Infantry Regiment of the Forty-fifth Infantry Division, part of a task force commanded by twenty-seven-year-old Colonel Felix Sparks, a Texas-born veteran of four amphibious landings in Europe. Shortly after Sparks had entered the Dachau complex that morning, around 11 A.M., men from the Forty-second Rainbow Division, under the command of Brigadier General Henning Linden, had arrived at the main entrance to Dachau and accepted the SS's formal surrender. Both groups of American soldiers had been ordered to secure the camp and to prevent inmates from exiting for fear of spreading disease and of reprisals against the local population.

Some inmates and liberators had already exacted vengeance on Germans within the Dachau complex itself. Inmates had stomped SS men to death and beaten others to a pulp with shovels and their fists.[82] The Americans had done little, if anything, to intervene. In one incident, Russian prisoners had grabbed a German by his legs and tore him apart, his bones cracking loudly. Some liberators, enraged by the horrors they found, had rounded up Waffen SS soldiers in an infirmary. Around midday, men from I Company of the 157th Infantry Regiment had lined up the SS soldiers in a coal yard and opened fire, killing at least eighteen men and wounding dozens more. By the time Levine arrived, the SS men's corpses lay, stiffening with rigor mortis, at the base of a wall in the coal yard.[83]

Later that afternoon of April 29, officers among the American liberators were shown key sites in the camp. As an intelligence officer, Levine would in all likelihood have been among those taken to the most brutal spots. In a nearby kennel lay the corpses of dozens of dogs, Dachau's infamous "Hounds from Hell" as one liberator described them.[84] Men from the Forty-fifth Thunderbird Infantry Division, which had spent over 500 days in combat since landing in Sicily on July 10, 1943, had killed the dogs, Dobermans and German shepherds, which a former camp commandant, Egon Zill, had painstakingly trained to savage prisoners strapped to metal poles.[85] Zill's fellow SS had then prodded the naked men's testicles with sticks. The dogs had quickly neutered their victims and were then rewarded with red meat.[86]

The dogs' corpses had joined hundreds upon hundreds of human ones littering the camp. Due to a shortage of coal, the SS had not been able to cremate the recent dead. So blue- and green-tinged carcasses lay piled in scores outside barracks and stacked to the ceilings in rooms near a crematorium.[87] Hundreds had died in the last few days. "Since all the many bodies were in various stages of decomposition," recalled one liberator, who had been among the first to enter the camp that day, "the stench of death was overpowering."[88]

In a kitchen near the dog pen, guards had prepared meals for the camp's canines. The meals were of far greater nutritional value than the thin cabbage soup and lumps of sawdust bread given to the inmates. There was also a crematorium in which around 100–150 people had been cremated each day. Then there were the gravel pits: countless enemies of the Reich had been shot here. Not far away was an embankment, and along its base was a ditch, covered by a wooden grating. Men were forced to kneel and then be shot. Their blood drained into the ditch. Some of their victims that spring had been German officers suspected of plotting against Hitler. They had been dispatched with a single shot in the back of the head.

At some point, Levine came across another group of survivors. They looked at him with "sick, large eyes" set back in their skulls. "You could see in many of them happiness at what they were seeing but [it was] the kind of happiness that reminded me of someone that was about to die and [still] had enough hearing to hear a pleasant sound," Levine recalled. "You had to concentrate carefully to see their smile, that there was pleasure in what they were either seeing or hearing."

Levine found it hard to continue looking at the survivors. Surely he could cope with what he was seeing? But then he realized he was not "handling things" as well as he wished. The more he looked at the survivors, the more he realized how terrible their torment had been: "The degree of sickness was unreal." Unless serious medical help arrived urgently, many of the inmates would perish. "People were dying of hunger but not so much as they were dying of typhus and the lack of medication." Strict orders had been given not to share any army rations with the inmates. "We [later] gave them food devised by the medical people," recalled Levine. "We thought food would be of great comfort, but it really wasn't. They couldn't handle it. They had been on such a starvation diet that they got sick because the food was too rich."[89]

Levine would later remember the immense suffering but also the unlimited gratitude of the liberated. Indeed, he would never forget how much the arrival of his fellow Americans in the camp meant to those who had waited for so long for freedom. A Pole named Walenty Lenarczyk, inmate no. 39272 at Dachau, later confirmed the immense joy of so many who had waited so long—for the "day of the Americans": "All we could think about were Americans. For the past six years we had waited for the Americans . . . It was truly our second birthday."[90]

IT WOULD BE A SLEEPLESS night for many men like Levine who had arrived at Dachau on April 29, 1945. The camp, according to one liberator, was "the most sickening and devastating thing we had ever experienced . . . The stench, the smell of death . . . permeated the air to the point that no one could eat his rations." One man's squad was assigned that night to guarding the camp's bakery to prevent any hunger-crazed inmates from raiding it. He was sick all night. "I don't think there was a guy who slept that night," he recalled, "and I don't think there was a guy who didn't cry openly that night."[91]

Now Levine and his fellow Liberators knew what they had been fighting for. As the *45th Infantry Division News* would soon declare in a headline above gruesome pictures, "This is why we fought." Unlike thousands of others who had died on the long journey to Germany, Levine and his fellow liberators had seen why the sacrifice had been necessary. "I've been in the army for 39 months," one man would tell a reporter. "I've been overseas in combat for 23. I'd gladly go through it all again if I knew that things like this would be stopped."[92]

The following morning, trucks loaded with food and medical supplies entered the camp, sent from Seventh Army supply depots.[93] The piles of dead bodies, green and yellow skinned, had not been removed. Many Americans who arrived at Dachau that day could not hold back the tears. "We cried not merely tears of sorrow," recalled Rabbi David Eichhorn, who arrived that morning.

"We cried tears of hate. Combat-hardened soldiers, Gentile and Jew, black and white, cried tears of hate."[94]

Another rabbi who entered Dachau on April 30 was Eli A. Bohnen with the Forty-second Rainbow Division. On May 1, 1945, he wrote to his wife,

> We entered the camp itself and saw the living. The Jews were the worst off. Many of them looked worse than the dead. They cried as they saw us. I spoke to a large group of Jews. I don't remember what I said, I was under such mental strain, but Heimberg (my assistant) tells me that they cried as I spoke. Some of the people were crying all the time we were there. They were emaciated, diseased, beaten, miserable caricatures of human beings. I don't know how they didn't all go mad. ... And as I said, the Jews were the worst. Even the other prisoners who suffered miseries themselves couldn't get over the horrible treatment meted out to the Jews.[95]

The man Levine had helped to a bunk, Maurice Pioro, was admitted to the 116th Evacuation Hospital on May 14, suffering from malnutrition. He would recover, unlike over 2,000 of his fellow inmates who had been liberated and would die that May in spite of the excellent care provided by U.S. Army doctors.[96] Almost 200 more would die that June, mostly from typhus.

Levine's fellow soldiers would eventually remove over 5,000 corpses from the Dachau complex.[97] Some of the bodies were buried with the "forced assistance" of local German civilians, some of whom would be made to handle the bodies.[98] Their willful blindness to the evil so close by would soon be the subject of much debate among not just Levine's comrades but also the shocked news correspondents who would visit the camp in coming weeks.[99]

In the days following liberation, Levine debriefed some of the inmates. He asked about their experience, how they were treated, under what circumstances they suffered, what they did for work, what food they had. Many years later, he stated that he wanted to debrief every person he came across inside the camp. He was fascinated by their pasts, how they had come to end up in Dachau. He heard of cases where the guards had taken prisoners into fields at night during bitterly cold weather and then hosed them down with ice-cold water, as they stood naked. They would be left to shiver all night: "The guards would return and most of those left outside would be dead by morning." Levine also remembered "many local residents [who] spoke of hearing anguished cries as the trains entered the camps and silence as they left."[100]

Levine learnt that German civilians were transported during the day to work in various factories or in the fields close to the Dachau complex. There were some who "lived right adjacent to the camp," recalled Levine. "You couldn't move out of the camp without running into some of [these] citizens."[101] German housewives tending their neat gardens would have been able to hear the sounds of people crying or screaming. "When people were taken to reach a factory or a field to work in, [they] didn't turn away," he added. "They had eyes and they had ears. Some of the SS personnel that administered the camp lived in the town."[102]

How could the Germans have been so callously indifferent to the suffering of so many people so close by? "Why didn't you do something?" Levine asked several civilians. "Why did you do all the things you were doing that supported or administered to the needs of that camp?" Levine recalled that,

Most felt they had no choice. That's what they would say. If they didn't comply, there would be reprisals against them. They would lose their livelihood. They might suffer some kind of incarceration or penalty . . . To say that the people of Dachau did not know what was going at in Dachau—there was no way. They did know . . . They couldn't bring themselves to admit their own weakness. I suppose a lot of people are like that. These people downplayed what they had heard and seen. If they had seen someone mistreated, for example hit with a rod, they told investigators that someone had been prodded. If they saw someone who was falling down sick, they would say perhaps to themselves that that person was maybe going to get help inside the camp where they had doctors.[103]

As an investigator, Levine was in his element, committed to gaining as much information as he possibly could. He recalled that sometimes, toward the end of an interview, he would "really stick it" to those being questioned if they were being evasive. It must, at times, have been almost impossible to contain his anger. Unlike locals from the town of Dachau, most inmates talked freely to him.[104] The problem was trying to verify things that prisoners said because "the imagination, time, pain and illness" often distorted their accounts. So Levine based his conclusions on many interviews, comparing accounts to corroborate stories.

Levine left Dachau at some point late that spring. He now had a chance to truly help some of the victims of Nazism, among them Jews. He was placed in charge of a German military barracks that was used as a displaced persons (DP) center, one of hundreds that sprang up in Germany to take care of some of the estimated 17 million DP in the country.[105] Among those housed in Levine's DP camp, according to one report, were around 5,000 Jews. Levine did what he could to care for them.[106] According to another account, he was "involved in feeding, clothing and eventually resettling more than 5,000 [of these] Holocaust survivors."[107]

Unlike many of his compatriots, Levine came to understand firsthand the enormity of Hitler's crimes in Europe. He would spend over a year in Germany, witnessing the first attempts at reconstruction as well as the appalling ruin, destitution, and

ALMOST 6 MILLION, OR TWO-THIRDS OF EUROPE'S PREWAR JEWISH POPULATION, HAD BEEN EXTERMINATED.

malnutrition that characterized much of the war-torn continent. In many areas, there was almost complete breakdown of law and order with widespread looting. Rape was epidemic. "[The] GI and Tommy have cigarettes and chocolate to give their Frauleins, so they need not rape," commented one Soviet soldier. "The Russian has neither."[108] Around 18 million Germans were homeless, many of them willing to do anything to find food, clothing, and warmth.

There had been vast moral as well as physical destruction. But none had suffered more than Europe's Jews. In one thing alone, Hitler had succeeded: rendering large swaths of the continent *Judenfrei*—free of Jews. Almost 6 million, or two-thirds of Europe's prewar Jewish population, had been exterminated. Ninety percent of Poland's Jews had died.[109] Among many of those still living, there was a hunger not for revenge but to abandon Europe altogether, and to make a new home in Palestine.

Levine finally returned to the U.S. in the summer of 1946 and was released from active duty a few months later. He arrived home with a footlocker containing the mementoes of a victor and photographs of what he had seen at Dachau. As with so many veterans who had seen the worst of the war, he was eager to put the past far behind him, indeed, to forget its horrors. He never mentioned the charnel house of Dachau to his family or friends. He dared not open the footlocker and set loose the demons he had stowed inside: "I never opened that footlocker for 38 years and never told my late wife or my children of any details of that event [Dachau] whatsoever—because it was more comfortable for me. Somehow I felt that they didn't need to know. Their life was comfortable and pleasant. There was no point."[110]

IN TEL AVIV, IN MAY 1985, Jewish veterans from around the globe gathered to commemorate the fortieth anniversary of the defeat of Nazi Germany. Among the honored guests from the United States was William P. Levine, on his first visit to the country.[111] On May 6, at Yad Vashem in Jerusalem, Levine attended an official opening ceremony of a memorial to Jewish veterans, military and civilian, who had fought the Nazis. Among a large crowd gathered at Yad Vashem that day was a balding fifty-seven-year-old former Red Army soldier. He recognized one of the honored guests. He moved closer and took a photograph of the man whose face he thought he had seen before. William P. Levine stared back. "He couldn't take his eyes off me," recalled the Red Army veteran. "I looked at him too but I didn't remember him from 40 years before. I didn't go up and speak to him because he was a general. I took photographs."[112]

Levine was seated between two Israeli government officials. The Red Army veteran finally decided to approach Levine.

"I know your face," said the veteran. "Didn't you fight against the Germans in the Second World War?"[113]

Levine said he had. "Wait for me after the celebrations," added Levine.[114]

Levine later found the veteran.

"[Levine] said he remembered me from somewhere but couldn't think where," recalled the veteran. "I told him I also remembered him but couldn't think where from."

Levine asked where the veteran had fought in the war.

"All the way from Stalingrad to Berlin."

Had the veteran been on the River Elbe? Leon Kotlowsky said that he had, just after a hard fight at an ammunition factory. Levine asked if he remembered an American who had spoken in Yiddish. Kotlowsky had indeed.

"I'm him," Levine said.

It was an extraordinary moment. The pair embraced. They shared memories of their last meeting, forty years before. Levine asked Kotlowsky to accompany him to a formal banquet. But Kotlowsky had to decline because he had to nurse his wife who was seriously ill. So they exchanged addresses instead, vowing to meet again.[115] Later that year, Kotlowsky arrived in Chicago. He was soon photographed clinking glasses in a toast to the Sabbath and friendship in Levine's home in Highland Park, Illinois.[116]

During Levine's stay in Israel, there had been another remarkable encounter. Again while at Yad Vashem in Jerusalem, another Jewish survivor of WWII had spotted Levine as Levine had addressed the crowd.[117] Levine finished speaking and began to walk away from the podium. A man ran over to Levine.

"General, don't you remember me?" asked the man.

Levine looked at him. "I'm sorry. I don't remember you."[118]

"When you came into Dachau," the man said, "I was lying in the agony of death and you lifted me up into your hands and you took care of me."[119]

Levine later vividly recalled meeting the man he had helped save at Dachau, four decades before: "Here was a man, grey-haired and in the bloom of life. He didn't look like the person that I could have possibly carried to that cot . . . His name was Maurice Pioro. A Belgian. He had compiled a book containing the names of all the Jews removed by the Nazis from Belgium and the date of their departure. He gave me that book as a memento of our having met again."[120]

Endnotes

1   William P. Levine archives, Pritzker Military Museum & Library.

2   Eulogy for Joseph A. Levine, 1888–1962, by Rabbi Raphael H. Levine, William P. Levine archives, Pritzker Military Museum & Library.

3   Eulogy for Joseph A. Levine.

4   United States Holocaust Memorial Museum, interview with William P. Levine, May 23, 1990 (hereafter, Levine interview 1990).

5   Officer's and Warrant Officer's Qualification Card, William P. Levine archives, Pritzker Military Museum & Library.

6   Dr. Waitman Beorn, "Preserving and Sharing Historic Firearms at the Pritzker Military Library." William P. Levine archives, Pritzker Military Museum & Library.

7   http://www.americanrhetoric.com/speeches/fdrpearlharbor.htm.

8   Enlistment record, William P. Levine archives, Pritzker Military Museum & Library.

9   Levine interview 1990.

10 Levine interview 1990.

11 Levine interview 1990.

12 http://articles.chicagotribune.com/2013-04-22/news/ct-met-general-levine-obit-20130422_1_levine-dachau-concentration-camp.

13 Leah Levine, personal diary, 1943. William P. Levine archives, Pritzker Military Museum & Library.

14 AAA Section, HQ 102D, Fourth Army, Louisiana, February 5, 1944, William P. Levine archives, Pritzker Military Museum & Library.

15 http://collections.ushmm.org/search/catalog/irn504623.

16 Levine interview 1990.

17 http://eisenhower.archives.gov/research/online_documents/d_day.html.

18 http://warchronicle.com/numbers/WWII/ddaycasualtyest.htm.

19 http://www.history.army.mil/books/wwii/100-11/ch5.htm.

20 Levine interview 1990.

21 Levine interview 1990.

22 *Pioneer Press*, June 3, 2004.

23 Levine interview 1990.

24 Levine interview 1990.

25 http://utah-musee-liberation.com/spip.php?article23.

26 http://www.historynet.com/from-d-day-to-paris-the-story-of-a-lifetime.htm.

27 http://alexkershawauthor.com/?p=155.

28 http://www.ushmm.org/wlc/en/article.php?ModuleId=10005458. See also Alex Kershaw, *The Envoy* (Cambridge, MA: Da Capo Press, 2010), p. 55.

29 http://www.yivoencyclopedia.org/article.aspx/Dnipropetrovsk.

30 http://alexkershawauthor.com/?p=155.

31 http://www.historynet.com/from-d-day-to-paris-the-story-of-a-lifetime.htm.

32 http://www.telegraph.co.uk/news/worldnews/northamerica/usa/7034587/Two-generals-bet-5-over-the-fate-of-Europe.html.

33 Johann Voss, letter to author, December 4, 2011.

34 http://www.historynet.com/ian-kershaws-the-end.htm.

35 Levine interview 1990.

36 Levine interview 1990.

37 Levine interview 1990.

38 Levine interview 1990.

39   Jack Lennard, "Jews in Wartime, 1939–45." William P. Levine archives,
     Pritzker Military Museum & Library.

40   Undated press cutting, William P. Levine archives, Pritzker Military Museum
     & Library.

41   G. I. Krivosheev, *Soviet Casualties and Combat Losses* (Greenhill, UK, 1997),
     p. 89.

42   Paul Robert Magocsi, *A History of Ukraine* (Toronto: University of Toronto
     Press, 1996), p. 633.

43   Undated press cutting, William P. Levine archives, Pritzker Military Museum
     & Library.

44   Wendy Morgan Lower, "From Berlin to Babi Yar: The Nazi War against the Jews,
     1941–44," *Journal of Religion and Society 9* (2007). Tens of thousands more
     would be killed at Babi Yar, including POWs and gypsies. Over 100,000 people
     had been killed at the site by the time Kotlowksy had arrived earlier that year.

45   Testimony of Leon Kotlowsky, in "Jews in Wartime 1939–45" by Jack Lennard,
     William P. Levine archives, Pritzker Military Museum & Library.

46   Testimony of Leon Kotlowsky.

47   Testimony of Leon Kotlowsky.

48   Testimony of Leon Kotlowsky.

49   http://www.jewishvirtuallibrary.org/jsource/ww2/jewstats.html.

50   "Jews in Wartime 1939–45."

51   Levine interview 1990.

52   Levine interview 1990.

53   Felix Sparks, 157th Infantry Regiment Newsletter, June 15, 1989.

54   *Denver Post*, August 26, 2001.

55   Marcus J. Smith, *Dachau: The Harrowing of Hell* (Albuquerque, 1972), p. 79.

56   Karl Mann, interview with author, 2011.

57   Felix Sparks, Regis University interview, 2003.

58   David Israel, *The Day the Thunderbird Cried* (Medford, OR: Emek Press,
     2005), p. 259.

59   John Lee, "Action at the Coal Yard Wall," *Second Platoon Newsletter*,
     April 2001, no. 20.

60   *Pioneer Press*, June 3, 2004.

61   *Pioneer Press*, June 3, 2004.

62   "Action at the Coal Yard Wall."

63   "Munich—Haupstadt der Bewegung," hrsg. Von Müncher Stadtmuseum,
     Munich, 1993, p. 244.

64 Pierre C.T. Verheye, *The Train Ride into Hell* (unpublished manuscript).

65 IfZ-Archiv, Nurnberger Dokumente, NO 2192, testimony of Hans Mehrbach, "The Death Train from Buchenwald."

66 "Eye Witness Report of Johann Bergmann, Buchenwald. Mahnung und Verpflichtung," Dokumente und Berichte (Berlin: Forth, 1983), pp. 503–5.

67 Dan Dougherty, interview with Jeffrey Hilton, 157th Infantry Regiment reunion, Colorado Springs, 2007.

68 Levine interview 1990. By the time he entered, some time that afternoon of April 29, there were very few actual SS guards in uniform within the camp. Most had already fled, having been warned of the American advance and having wisely chosen to disappear. "The arrival of US forces was not concealed well," recalled Levine. The guards had clearly been aware of the possibility, as he would later put it, that "they wouldn't fare very well if they were still in the camp when we arrived." Revenge might be swiftly dealt from "two sources", Levine would add, "from us—the soldiers—and also from the inmates" (Levine interview 1990).

69 Levine interview 1990.

70 Levine interview 1990.

71 Levine interview 1990.

72 Levine interview 1990.

73 Levine interview 1990.

74 Levine interview 1990.

75 William Levine, speech at Chicago Holocaust Memorial Day, 1995. William P. Levine archives, Pritzker Military Museum & Library.

76 Levine interview 1990. According to Levine, this man would later become the "head of the Belgian delegation of the International Convention of Ghetto Fighters and Jewish Resistance Fighters from the Second World War" (Levine interview 1990)

77 Speech by Levine, Chicago Holocaust Memorial Day, William P. Levine archives, Pritzker Military Museum & Library.

78 Speech by Levine.

79 Speech by Levine.

80 Jack Hallowell, *Eager for Duty* (n.p., n.d.), p. 167.

81 *Chicago Tribune*, April 30, 1945.

82 I.G. Whitaker, Report, Walenty Lenarczyk testimony, p. 51, National Archives.

83 *New Orleans Times Picayune*, May 27, 2001.

84 After Action Report, 157th Infantry Regiment, 45th Division, National Archives.

85 Hermann Weiss, Dachau and International Public Opinion, Reactions to the

Liberation of the Camp, (1987), p. 34.

86　Dachau and Nazi Terror, 1933–1945, Studies and Reports (Dachau, 2002), p. 34. The dogs had died quickly, howling and whimpering as the Thunderbirds gunned them down. One soldier had apparently used a dagger to cut a dog's throat after it had been shot but stubbornly did not die. Just one of the dogs would survive to be found a week later with a bullet wound, hiding in an SS barracks.

87　According to Nerin E. Gun, *The Day of the Americans* (New York: Fleet Publishing, 1966), p. 64, "A week later a GI pilfering in one of the abandoned SS barracks, heard a growling coming from behind some cases in a dark corner. He approached cautiously and was startled to see a German Shepherd dog—his head was bloody from a bullet wound. The animal had apparently been hiding there without food and water for several days, licking his wound. The GI ran away and no one knows what happened to the wretched animal."

88　Emajean Buechner, *Sparks: The Combat Diary of a Battalion Commander* (Metairie, LA: Thunderbird Press, 1991), p. 142.

89　Levine interview 1990.

90　//www.scrapbookpages.com/DachauScrapbook/DachauLiberation/ LiberationDay3C.html.

91　John Lee, interviewed by James Strong, "The Liberation of KZ Dachau," 1990.

92　*45th Infantry Division News*, May 1945.

93　157th Infantry Regiment, After Action Report, April 1945, National Archives.

94　Dachau and the Nazi Terror, Testimonies, I, Verlag Dachauer Hefte gGmbH, 2002, p. 53.

95　http://www.scrapbookpages.com/DachauScrapbook/DachauLiberation/ LiberationDay3C.html.

96　Maurice Pioro, medical report, William P. Levine archives, Pritzker Military Museum & Library Library.

97　http://www.scrapbookpages.com/DachauScrapbook/DachauLiberation/ aftermath.html.

98　Felix Sparks, Regis University lecture.

99　Felix Sparks, Regis University lecture.

100　William P. Levine, Holocaust Memorial Day Speech, Chicago, 1995. William P. Levine archives, Pritzker Military Museum & Library.

101　Levine interview 1990.

102　Levine interview 1990.

103　Levine interview 1990.

104 Levine interview 1990.

105 Keith Lowe, *Savage Continent* (New York: Picador, 2013), p. 27.

106 Orah Arif, "It Was Too Terrible for Me to Want to Remember," William P. Levine archives, Pritzker Military Museum & Library.

107 http://articles.chicagotribune.com/2013-04-22/news/ct-met-general-levine-obit-20130422_1_levine-dachau-concentration-camp.

108 Major A.G. Moon, Imperial War Museum Docs, 06/126/I, typescript memoir, p. 56

109 https://www.jewishvirtuallibrary.org/jsource/Holocaust/killedtable.html.

110 Arif, "It Was Too Terrible for Me to Want to Remember.".

111 Arif, "It Was Too Terrible for Me to Want to Remember."

112 Arif, "It Was Too Terrible For Me To Want To Remember."

113 *Jewish Chronicle*, November 29, 1985.

114 Testimony of Leon Kotlowsky.

115 Testimony of Leon Kotlowsky.

116 *Chicago Tribune*, undated press cutting, William P. Levine archives, Pritzker Military Museum & Library. Dachau and Its Liberation," 157th Infantry Association Newsletter, March 20, 1984.

117 http://patch.com/illinois/highlandpark/obituary-major-general-william-p-levine.

118 Levine interview 1990.

119 Arif, "It Was Too Terrible for Me to Want to Remember."

120 Levine interview 1990.

ALBUM

★ ★

Images from a Military Life

★ ★

■ William Levine, shown here with his three younger brothers, grew up in the Lake Superior port town of Duluth, Minnesota, where in the 1920s, his Russian immigrant father Joseph (at rear) operated this small grocery store.

■

After Officer Candidate School in the spring of '43, new Second Lieutenant Levine enjoyed a day at the beach in North Carolina.

Below, Levine's "Enlistment Record" notes that when he was drafted in August 1942 he was already married.

Entering the army, Levine bade goodbye to wife Leah and left his job for basic training at Fort Bliss, Texas.

❝ *...We had hopes of leaving today but when Wm went to Col. (James?) to get his papers, the Col. told him that he had rec'd a wire from Camp Davis to hold Wm until further notice. The Col had sent them a recommendation to commission Wm as a Lt. without attending O.C.S. Wow! What a thrill that would be."* **—From the diary of Leah Levine**

Thursday, May 13, 1943

The Day was gorgeous. Sunny and blue skies. Met Bucky at 8 and went over to see the parade and graduation. I was thrilled to tears especially when I saw Lt. William. I was barely jumping out of my skin.

We left Wilmington at 2:30 on the Charlotte bus. Had a flat tire 30 mi. from town. Were treated to Southern hospitality. A woman by the side of the road bought cokes for us all.

■ Leah, who kept a daily diary through 1943, noted OCS graduation day and their departure from Wilmington.

■ William and Leah at his graduation from Antiaircraft OCS at Camp Davis near Wilmington, NC.

■ At the close of
World War II, Captain
William Levine enjoys
a light moment with
an artillery buddy.

■ As a Lieutenant Colonel, Levine took
many advanced army training courses
at bases around the country.

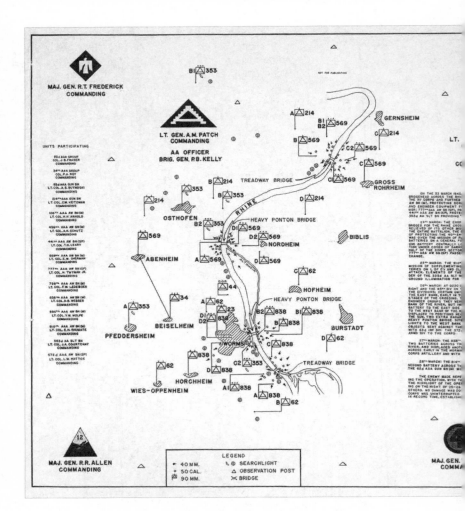

■ Protecting the Seventh U.S. Army's crossing of the Rhine into Germany on two pontoon bridges, antiaircraft batteries were positioned on the west bank. Levine's 45th Division crossed near Nordheim.

> **Hitler's hold on power was still unassailable, his fanatical followers legion, ordinary citizens prepared to endure to the bitter end, victims of propaganda, self-delusion, and the extraordinary apparatus of terror that the SS and Gestapo had zealously created under SS Reichsfuhrer Heinrich Himmler."** —Alex Kershaw

■ The 1918 Ludendorff Bridge, near Remagen was captured intact by the U.S. Ninth Armored Division in March 1945 when the Germans failed to demolish it; an American bridgehead was quickly established.

1 C 5 CEC

Army of the United States

SEPARATION QUALIFICATION RECORD
SAVE THIS FORM. IT WILL NOT BE REPLACED IF LOST

This record of job assignments and special training received in the Army is furnished to the soldier when he leaves the service. In its preparation, information is taken from available Army records and supplemented by personal interview. The information about civilian education and work experience is based on the individual's own statements. The veteran may present this document to former employers, prospective employers, representatives of schools or colleges, or use it in any other way that may prove beneficial to him.

1. LAST NAME—FIRST NAME—MIDDLE INITIAL	MILITARY OCCUPATIONAL ASSIGNMENTS		
LEVINE WILLIAM P	10. MONTHS	11. GRADE	12. MILITARY OCCUPATIONAL SPECIALTY
2. ARMY SERIAL NO. / 3. GRADE / 4. SOCIAL SECURITY NO.	11	Capt	Supply and Evacuation Staff Officer (4010)
0-1055895 Major Unknown			
5. PERMANENT MAILING ADDRESS (Street, City, County, State)	26	Capt	Intelligence Officer (9301)
1221 N. Queen Avenue Minneapolis, Hennepin County, Minn.			
6. DATE OF ENTRY INTO ACTIVE SERVICE / 7. DATE OF SEPARATION / 8. DATE OF BIRTH			
13 May 1943 15 Sep 1946 1 Jul 1915			
9. PLACE OF SEPARATION			
SEPARATION CENTER, FORT DIX, N.J.			

SUMMARY OF MILITARY OCCUPATIONS

13. TITLE—DESCRIPTION—RELATED CIVILIAN OCCUPATION

SUPPLY AND EVACUATION STAFF OFFICER: Served with 34th Anti-Aircraft Artillery Group in the European Theater of Operations. Was responsible for coordination, procurement and issue of all types of supplies for 10 battalions. Was responsible for supplies for 75,000 war criminals in hospitals, camps, and prisons.

INTELLIGENCE OFFICER: Was responsible for dissemination, gathering, evaluation and collation of information regarding the enemy and enemy capabilities as would affect the operations of United States Army. Was also responsible for Anti-Aircraft Artillery Intelligence Service with 15th Corps, 7th Army.

WD AGO form 100
1 JUL 1945

This form supersedes WD AGO Form 100, 15 July 1944, which will not be used.

■ Major Levine's forty months of regular army service ended in September 1946 with this official summary of his assignments, which included responsibility for a large number of POWs .

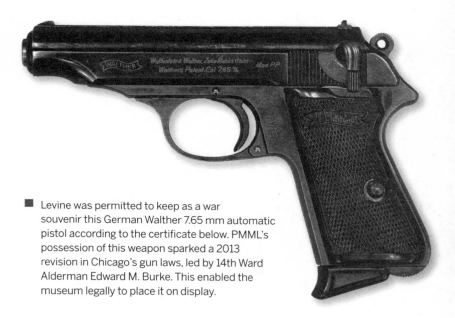

Levine was permitted to keep as a war souvenir this German Walther 7.65 mm automatic pistol according to the certificate below. PMML's possession of this weapon sparked a 2013 revision in Chicago's gun laws, led by 14th Ward Alderman Edward M. Burke. This enabled the museum legally to place it on display.

CERTIFICATE

1 June 46
(Date)

1.   I certify that I have personally examined the items of captured enemy equipment in the possession of _WILLIAM P. LEVINE, CAPT_ and that the bearer is officially authorized by the Theater Commander, under the provisions of Sec VI, Cir 155, WD, 28 May 1945, to retain as his personal property the articles listed in Par 3, below.

2.   I further certify that if such items are to be mailed to the US, they do not include any items prohibited by Sec VI, Cir 155, WD, 28 May 1945.

3.   The items referred to are :

1 WALTHER PISTOL 7.65 mm
311 538

2 Clips

J.C. Fredenick
(Signature)

Lt Col CAC, 133d AAA Gun Bn
(Rank, Branch and Organization)

(This certificate will be prepared in duplicate)

AG USFET Form N° 33

Lef. 8-45 5.000,000 78,920

47

■ Among Levine's papers was this U.S. Army medical record of Maurice Pioro, the prisoner Levine had encountered and aided two weeks earlier when he first entered the Nazi camp.

■ Surviving Dachau prisoners cheered the American soldiers when they liberated the camp in April 1945 (top). The last German POWs held there were released and left the camp at the end of June 1945 (bottom).

■ Levine, center, worked in Chicago as president of Lakeside Plastics Sales Co. for about thirty years. His brother, Orrin, is second from left; cousin Zelman Levine is third from left.

■ Below, a 1950s postcard of Fort Sheridan, a military training center where Levine spent USAR time for many years.

Headquarters Row, Fort Sheridan, Ill.

■ Left, Leah Levine at home with her children, John and Maxine, in 1958.

■ In February 1957 Levine assumed command of the 383rd Antiaircraft Artillery Gun Battalion, whose key weapon was the M51 Skysweeper.

■

Right: A page from Levine's military record showing army service-school courses he took from the 1940s until 1962.

```
Change of Command - 21 November 1970

LTC Harold T. Cooney      Retiring Bn Cdr
MAJ GEN Wm P Levine
MAJ George E. Elliott     New BN Cdr
MAJ Clifton G. Carle      X.O.

On line as "Pass IN Review"
```

■

Above and right: Major General Levine in olive khakis and at a change of command ceremony at Fort McCoy, Wisconsin, in 1970, when he was commanding officer of the 85th Division (Training).

❝ *He wanted to understand military objectives and what would be needed for his unit to succeed. His men, individually and as a unit, always knew that he had their interests at heart."* —John Levine, **William's son**

4. DATE OF BIRTH	5. RACE	6. DATE OF CURRENT TOUR	7. RELIGION	8. BRANCH	
				BASIC	CONTROL
1 Jul 15	CAU	—	Jewish	GO	—

15.	RATINGS, SPECIALTIES AND DESIGNATIONS		
TYPE		DATE	AUTHORITY

16.	CIVILIAN EDUCATION AND MILITARY SCHOOLING			
SCHOOL	MAJOR OR COURSE	DURAT.	COMP.	YEAR
Duluth Central (HS)	Academic	4 yrs	Dipl	33
Univ Of Minn (Col)	Psychol.-Zoology	3½ yrs	No	36
AA Sch Cp Davis N.C.	AA Off Cand	13 wks	Yes	43
AAFSAT, Orlando, Fla	Staff Off	2 wks	Yes	43
I&E Staff Sch, Paris	Instructor Tng	2 wks	Yes	45
Le Mans, France	Bomb Recon	2 wks	Yes	45
Epernay, France	Mine-Booby Trap	2 wks	Yes	45
5902 USAR Sch, Chicago	C&GS (Phase I)	1 yr	Yes	51
	(Phase II)	1 yr	Yes	52
	(Adv(Phase III)	1 yr	Yes	53
	(Adv Phase IV)	1 yr	Yes	54
	(Adv Phase V)	1 yr	Yes	55
5907 USAR Sch FtSheridan	C&GS	2 wks	Yes	54
5903 USARSch Ft Riley Kan	C&GS	2 wks	Yes	55
ICAF	NatResourcesConf	23days	Yes	56
Educ Equiv-AIOC-Arty				
C&GS USAR Assoc Course		5 yrs	Yes	53
C&GS Ft Leavenworth Kan	Ph I nuc WpnCrse		Yes	62
Arty&MslSchFtSillOkla	PH IINucWpnCrse	2 wks	Yes	62
USASWS Ft Bragg N.C.	Sr Off Orien	1 wk	Yes	62

❝ *Your function as a division commander is, first, to instill a sense of urgency and focus on the mission of the unit, which was to train soldiers for combat. Everything focused on that—to train soldiers to defend our nation. As a division commander, your job was to make sure your unit understood the mission, was equipped to do the mission and could execute the mission."* —James Mukoyama, former division captain of the Eighty-fifth

■ Major General Levine during a training exercise at an undisclosed base.

■ Lieutenant General John H. Michaelis, U.S. Fifth Army commander, pins a second star on newly promoted Major General William Levine, with help from wife Leah, in May 1967. Levine was then commander of the USAR 84th Division.

■ Levine and Rhoda Kreiter at a social function in 1978. They would marry two years later.

6/9/85

· Dear general.
As you can see I send to you six pictures that I shot
in Jerusalem and in TEL-AVIV. I am not a proffesional
photographer but, it is my holby, and I did my best that thy
will be in high quality.
In order to memorize forty years of our victory on the
German S.S, I shoot those pictures for the jornal of
the Israeli veterance organization.
I want to remind you in few words our meeting in the
Elba river in April 26 1945.
Than I was vice comander (captur) of the tank regiment
in the polish military under the Russian command. It was
our last battle in the war. This battle took place in a
small village, which a big amunition factory was in
there. In this village, the SS devission destroied us
six tanks. Afterwards, after a heavy fighty we
succeded to destroy the enemy, and we came to the
elba river. Than in the other side of the river we
saw the American forces. A group of the American officiers
... tka and vski·
... than major from the
... knew a little german
... I was the translater.
... that I talk with a

e were
t this place.
a lot of
wife is very
the her, be
ther as you
help of
Kenesst

son who
while I

g writing to
ski LEON
DRUT ST.
8

o 835.

■ Levine and former Polish soldier Leon Kotlowsky, who met when U.S. and
Soviet troops mingled at the River Elbe in 1945, were reunited at a ceremony
for Jewish veterans in Tel Aviv in 1985. Kotlowsky later wrote this letter to Levine.

Thirty eight years after their encounter at Dachau in 1945, freed prisoner Maurice Pioro inscribed this memorial book (right) about the deportation of Belgian jews to his liberator, William P. Levine.

MÉMORIAL DE LA DÉPORTATION DES JUIFS DE BELGIQUE

présenté par
Serge KLARSFELD et
Maxime STEINBERG

C'était une grande joie pour moi de vous rencontrer 38 après la libération de Dachau.

Le Mémorial à Anderlecht a été inauguré le 19 avril 1970 par les plu religieuses de notre pays. On avait enfin trouvé un lieu de pèler

Mais après le procès de Kiel qui nous a, en tant que partie civile, e du Ministère de la Santé Publique et de la Famille, il était de notre d les noms de tous nos martyrs, afin que chaque famille juive ait

Le procès de Kiel, mettant au banc des accusés les principaux re de Belgique, a pu avoir lieu grâce à la vigilance de Serge et de B Maxime Steinberg et à la collaboration active sur le terrain de n

Ce recueil constitue un témoignage ineffaçable de l'exterminati distribué aux bibliothèques du monde entier pour combattre la

Ce mémorial est dédié à la mémoire des cinquante millions c seconde guerre mondiale, à la mémoire de nos six millions de 23.838 Juifs de Belgique qui ont été déportés de la caserne Dossi tion et qui n'en sont pas revenus. Nous devons nous souvenir d ment page après page, de ces êtres humains qui furent assass Juifs. Hommes, femmes et enfants dont les cendres furent épa

Il est dédié à tous ceux qui, au péril de leur vie, ont sauvé quelqu trois mille enfants.

Il est dédié à toutes ces communautés juives de Pologne et d'au disparu et dont les survivants sont venus renforcer notre comm mondiale.

Je souhaite m'adresser ici aux jeunes, aux Fils et Filles de la Dé dire combien je suis rassuré de savoir qu'ils reprennent le fla combattre la négation de l'Holocauste afin que jamais plus il

> ❝ *By then Levine had fulfilled what he considered his final mission: telling people about war and about hatred and about Dachau, so they could work to ensure that it doesn't happen again. 'The world cannot survive another event such as the Holocaust,' Levine said in one interview. 'It can't. We will all lose our humanity.'"*—**Richard Ernsberger, Jr.**

■

The Moriah Congregation in Deerfield, Illinois (background), dedicated this plaque to Levine as thanks for his service to the temple. It is attached to a rock in a small outside garden.

■ On his U.S. Army Reserve retirement in July 1975, Levine was lauded for his "outstanding personal example, professionalism and selfless dedication," and he received the Distinguished Service Medal.

PART TWO

The Postwar Years
Memories of the Liberation

BY RICHARD ERNSBERGER, JR.

L evine returned to the United States in the summer of
1946 and was released from active duty soon after.
Like every other American soldier who'd survived a
brutal war, he was eager to resume his civilian life. The
war was hell for the troops but a tremendous catalyst for the
American economy, which was in the early stages of what would
become a prolonged postwar boom. Good jobs awaited the men
coming home. So did family and friends—parents, siblings, wives,
girlfriends, children. After a period of hardship and combat,
after defeating the Germans and Japanese, American military
personnel and civilians alike sought a return to normalcy.

William and Leah Levine had been apart longer than they'd
been together as husband and wife. The couple settled into an
apartment in Minneapolis, Leah's hometown. The two were
familiar with the city, 150 miles south of Duluth; both had
attended the University of Minnesota before the war. That's where
they'd met. Levine, then thirty-one, brought home a footlocker
containing army paraphernalia—the mementoes of a victor. But
he wasn't in a mood to open it. As with so many veterans, he
wanted to forget the war and its horrors. He never mentioned
the charnel house of Dachau to Leah or anyone else in his family.

He found a sales position with a local clothing company, but
it wouldn't last long. By then the small plastics firm started in the
1930s by a first cousin, Zelman Levine, Duluth-based Lakeside
Plastics, had achieved some success. It was a family operation:
two of William's three brothers—his twin, Clarence, and youngest
brother, Orrin—were among various relatives working for
the firm, which specialized in designing and making point-of-
sale advertising displays for retail establishments. Breweries

were the chief customers for the signs, which they installed in bars and restaurants. Clarence would eventually manage the manufacturing side of the business—and Levine's third brother, Robert, a watchmaker by trade, would later join the company too.

Aiming to broaden the company's customer base, the men decided to open a sales office in Chicago. William liked that idea and decided to join the firm, and then he and Orrin moved to Chicago to set up the new operation. They secured an office at 407 South Dearborn Street, in downtown Chicago, and Lakeside Plastics Sales Co. was launched. William traveled almost

HE NEVER MENTIONED THE
CHARNEL HOUSE OF DACHAU TO LEAH
OR ANYONE ELSE IN HIS FAMILY.

every week, throughout the United States, visiting current or prospective clients. Thanks in large part to its new sales arm, Lakeside Plastics, while not huge, would grow steadily over the next three decades and eventually go public.

William and Leah, meanwhile, found an apartment in the Rogers Park neighborhood in the far northeastern corner of Chicago, alongside Lake Michigan. The neighborhood, home to Loyola University, had become an attractive destination for ethnic Irish, German, English, and Jewish families seeking relief from the crowded city center—or, in some cases, from devastated Europe. It was a nice spot for a couple whose forebears came from eastern Europe—William's from Russia and Lithuania and Leah's from Belarus.

Leah, kind and supportive by nature, was comfortable with the move—and ready, with her husband, to start a family. Before long they would have two children, both born in Chicago—Maxine, in 1949, and John, in 1951. It was a happy time for the couple. "They had a very special relationship," recalls daughter Maxine (Levine) Souza, who lives in Buffalo Grove, Illinois. "They were devoted to each other. Every day he came home from work, she would run to the door and hug and kiss him, as if he'd been gone for years." (Given that he had been gone for years, during the war, it was an understandable instinct.) "It was amazing: a big hug and a kiss—it wasn't just a peck—every single day."

When he was discharged from active service, Levine was sure that his military days were over. At least that's what he told an interviewer later in his life. But he apparently enjoyed military life more than he was willing to admit, for not long after his return to America Levine joined the U.S. Army Reserve (USAR), the peacetime pool of trained military officers and enlisted men who could be mobilized in time of war. Together with the Army National Guard, the reserve constitutes the army's reserve component of the U.S. armed forces. The USAR was first organized under the 1920 National Defense Act, following World War I, when Congress reorganized U.S. land forces by authorizing a regular army, a national guard, and an organized reserve, which later became the USAR.

These days the USAR has some 205,000 reserve officers and soldiers, who are required to serve at least thirty-nine days annually—one weekend every month at a base for training and two weeks of active duty. Officers typically put in significantly more hours, depending on rank and responsibilities. As he had in the regular army, Levine would flourish in the reserve over the next thirty years, between 1946 and 1975, steadily rising in rank even as he worked at his sales job and, with Leah, raised a family. He would eventually become a highly respected one- and then two-star division commander and a belated local spokesman for the terror of the Holocaust.

Why stay with the military? Levine said that he became convinced, near the end of World War II, that the United States would soon be fighting again—this time against Russia. While in Switzerland, he recalled, civilians frequently asked him, "When is the United States going to fight Russia or China? I was asked that question so many times in so many places that I became convinced that they all couldn't be wrong. I felt that the Russians would be our target."

He himself considered Russia, under Stalin, untrustworthy. Immediately after Germany's capitulation, the U.S. military began sending displaced persons back to Eastern Europe by train. When the trains would get to the borders of Poland and Yugoslavia, said Levine, Russian soldiers would stop and board the trains and take everything of value from the displaced persons and then force the train to turn around and return to Germany. "We started to put armed guards on the trains," recalled Levine, one of whom at one point shot and killed a Russian soldier. It wasn't hard to envision a war against the ruthless Stalin, who had been America's ally in the fight against Hitler. "I didn't want to be discharged and then be recalled and have to start [my military career] again."

Jonathan Plotkin, the husband of one Levine's three step-daughters by his second wife, mentioned a couple of other reasons why he would have wanted to stay in the military. For one thing, said Plotkin, "He felt that the service was an important part of his identity." Later in life, he would talk to students about his military career and emphasize "the importance of being vigilant and being a patriot and doing what you had to do—going back to the militia days in colonial America, when you dropped your hoe and picked up your musket and defended your family." Plotkin says that Levine also once mentioned, with a grin, that he wanted to outrank some of the jerks of higher rank that he encountered while in the army. "He wanted to eventually outrank them. I think he said that tongue-in-cheek, but he did not suffer fools gladly."

LEVINE'S FIRST NOTABLE position in the reserves was serving as S3 for the 383rd AAA (antiaircraft artillery) Battalion in Chicago from 1949 to 1950. Military unit officers have specific headquarters responsibilities. Staffers at a division headquarters are given a G designation, while those at smaller brigade and battalion headquarters are designated with an S. A G1 (or S1) handles personnel and administrative matters, a G2 (or S2) is responsible for intelligence, a G3 (or S3) manages training and operations, and a G4 (or S4 handles) logistics. Of the four, the 3 section leader "is considered the most important and requires your best staffer," says Major General (retired) James Mukoyama, who once served under Levine in the reserves.

An S3 has numerous duties. Among them, he or she must determine the training needs of the unit, plan and write the operational orders that must be carried out by battalions and companies, coordinate the activities and operations of the unit with other members of the command staff (logistics, intelligence), develop training plans, and, above all, work to ensure unit readiness, which would include ammunition supply and the operating quality of field equipment.

Major Levine, as an S3, would have managed a small section staff of his own and worked closely with the artillery battalion's executive officer. As one former sergeant put it, "It may often be the case that the S3 officer knows more about what the battalion as a whole can do than the CO [Commanding Officer], who, fairly, must split his attention across his entire unit." Put simply, S3 is a big job and one that requires smarts and leadership skills.

In subsequent years, Major Levine was assigned to different units but stayed close to home—his responsibilities rising along with his rank. He next served as an S3 and S2 with the 374th AAA, also based in Chicago, and then was transferred to the 5902nd USAR school in Chicago, where he was got intelligence training. In August 1955, Levine was appointed lieutenant colonel and became Executive Officer of the 308th Military Government Group. Two years later he assumed command of the 383rd AAA Gun Battalion (Skysweeper). A USAR battalion would typically comprise 400–500 soldiers.

The Skysweeper was a relatively new surface-to-air anti-aircraft weapon whose radar system was integrated, for the first time, with the gun and fire-control systems. Deployed by both the army and air force, the Skysweeper had a range of four miles and could fire forty-five rounds a minute. It was the last of the military's conventional AAA guns. The weapon had some tactical issues (it was not easily hidden, to name one) and would be phased out quickly in favor of the more powerful Nike missile systems introduced in the 1950s.

After his short stint with the Skysweeper battalion, Levine became commanding officer of the Seventh Howitzer Battalion, Third Artillery, based in Evanston, Illinois. In 1960 came another bump up the military ladder when he was named executive officer of the XIV Corps Artillery and later was made assistant commander of that unit.

Levine, late in his life, told an interviewer that he'd traveled to Korea "off and on" in the early 1950s, during the Korean War. He had units there, he said, and went for a couple of weeks or a couple of months to monitor their performance. Nothing could be found in his military record indicating when, specifically, he might have made such trips, and there is scant information nowadays about the AAA units with which he was associated in the 1950s. None seem to be listed among those antiaircraft battalions that participated in the Korean War.

As a veteran artillery officer, Levine would have been quite familiar with the sights and sounds of an AAA battery. As described in a 1953 article in the *Antiaircraft Journal*, there would be "long-barreled 90mm guns slanting toward the sky, olive-drab trailers, sand-bagged revetments, and radar antennas turning and turning again, searching from horizon to horizon [for enemy aircraft]." An artillery or AAA unit might comprise ordnance, engineering, signal, and quartermaster teams. The proper maintenance and timely repair of the guns and other equipment, the husbanding of ordnance and general safeguarding against loss and damage—all were commander priorities.

As *Antiaircraft Journal* pointed out in 1953, for an AAA battery "the days are long and sometimes tedious... Life is a seemingly endless succession of tracking missions, of drill with dummy ammunition, of watching and waiting and searching the empty sky. But at day's end there is time for fun and relaxation and for the good-natured horseplay you'll always find whenever a group of healthy, high-spirited young men get together . . ."

A RESERVIST, AND IN PARTICULAR a reserve officer, must be a "juggler," says Jim Mukoyama. He or she has to balance three life commitments—to one's family, to one's commercial job, and to the military (army reserve), which for officers means an extensive time commitment. For one thing, officers typically attend midweek "administrative drills" at their headquarters, which essentially are planning sessions for the next so-called Battle Assembly—the once-a-month weekend of training. "A unit can't just function by meeting once a month," says Mukoyama. "Things happen throughout the month, and you have to continually stay abreast of different things that are going on in the military—new doctrine, new equipment and, as you get promoted in rank, there are new military education requirements."

Levine, like his colleagues, spent various periods in the 1950s and 1960s, pen and notebook in hand, taking military classes that were relatively short in duration. Between 1951 and 1955 he took a series of Associate Command and General Staff College courses taught in Chicago, at Fort Riley, Kansas, and at Fort Sheridan, Illinois. In addition, in 1954, he spent twenty-three days at the Industrial College of the Armed Forces at Fort Blair, in Washington, D.C. It was established in 1924, with help from Wall Street investor Bernard Baruch, to focus on wartime procurement and mobilization issues. Nowadays, it trains military officers and civilians for senior national security positions and in 2012 was renamed the Dwight D. Eisenhower School for National Security and Resource Strategy. In 1957 Levine attended the U.S. Army Air Defense School at Fort Bliss, Texas. In 1959 he was awarded credit for the Associate Artillery Battery Officers' Course. In 1962, Lieutenant Colonel Levine attended Artillery and Missile School and took a Nuclear Weapons Employment course—one at Fort Leavenworth, Kansas, the other at Fort Sill, Oklahoma, and a year later he also took a one-week U.S. Army Unconventional Warfare Orientation course at Fort Bragg, North Carolina. And, finally, in 1967 he completed a two-week Senior Officer course at the U.S. Army War College in Carlyle, Pennsylvania. Military technologies, tactics, and policies evolve steadily, and officers and soldiers must keep pace.

Unsurprisingly, army personnel and reservists move around a lot. During his long USAR career, Levine's two-week active-duty stints took him and the troops all over the country—to Fort Bliss, Fort Hood, and Fort Sam Houston, all in Texas; to Fort Meyer, Fort Belvoir, and Fort Lee, in Virginia; to Fort Campbell, Kentucky; Fort Benning, Georgia; Fort Lewis, Washington; Fort Polk, Louisiana; Fort Leonard Wood, Missouri; Fort Ord, California; and Fort McCoy, Wisconsin, among others. "Depending on the year, he was in lots of different places," recalls his son, John. "When he had the artillery unit, they shot guns at summer camp."

ALL OF THAT MAKES IT EASY to forget that the army reserve is a second job. Levine still had his busy schedule as a salesman for Lakeside Plastics—and in the early 1950s he became a commuter man. In 1953 he and Leah moved with their two children to the city of Highland Park, Illinois, an affluent North Shore bedroom community twenty-seven miles north of Chicago, on the western edge of Lake Michigan in Lake County. Highland Park, which has about 30,000 residents today, went through two boom periods— first in the 1920s and then in the 1950s, fueled by families looking for a respite from urban stress.

The city has a significant Jewish population, and that is one reason Major Levine chose to live there. Jewish families began gravitating to Highland Park in the first half of the twentieth century partly because of its scenic beauty, partly because it was affordable (although that is not a word that would describe the North Shore today), and partly to avoid the discriminatory practices then common in Chicago and some suburbs. The prominent "prairie-style" landscape architect Jens Jenson, who did a lot of work for Henry and Edsel Ford in the 1920s and 1930s, lived in Highland Park, as did architects Howard Van Doren Shaw and Robert Seyfarth. The Chicago Symphony Orchestra has made Highland Park's popular Ravinia Festival its summer home since 1936. Ravinia, a village within Highland Park, was originally an artists' colony. The film director John Hughes filmed location shots for several of his 1980s hit movies, including *Home Alone* and *Ferris Bueller's Day Off*, in Highland Park. Also to be found in the city is the iconic Willits House, designed by Frank Lloyd Wright in 1901 and considered the first great example of so-called prairie-style architecture.

Levine bought a contemporary ranch house on two acres at 560 Green Bay Road and there settled with his family. "Maxine and I were raised in that house, which he kept until 1980," says

John Levine, a resident of Northbrook, Illinois, who had a career in corporate marketing and now writes children's books. Most days Levine took the train into downtown Chicago, to his job. By all accounts, he liked sales and at some point in his career became president of the Point of Purchase Advertising Institute.

John Levine recalls his father taking him and his sister Maxine to work with him on Columbus Day in 1959. John was eight years old at the time, Maxine, ten. "I remember emerging from the Northwestern Station in downtown Chicago and the three of us making our way through a sea of commuters." The three hustled along Jackson Boulevard. "I struggled to keep up with Dad," says John, "who was striding ahead with confidence and urgency." After getting to the office, the kids watched TV in a conference room, surrounded by colorful, electric point-of-sale signs on the four walls. At noon Levine and the children had lunch at the Maple Leaf restaurant—burgers, fries, and chocolate shakes for John and Maxine, soup with Ry-Krisp for Dad.

As a parent, Levine was stern but magnanimous, and John points to a childhood incident as an example. One morning in 1956, when John and Maxine were small childern, they grabbed crayons and started drawing on the concrete mantel over the fireplace in the living room. "We were doing our Diego Rivera impression," says John. When his mother discovered the drawings, she was furious. "But my dad laughed it off. He said he wouldn't think of removing the scribbles and wanted to keep them there as a reminder of his adorable young children." The crayon doodles stayed on the fireplace mantel until the house was sold.

Maxine (Levine) Souza, who has an administrative job at Harper Community College in Palatine, Illinois, says that her father wasn't always such a soft touch. "He was very determined, meticulous—he wanted things done the right way. He was very loving but had high expectations." Within the household, she says, "there was a lot of structure and routine." She and her brother attended Ravinia Elementary School and then, later, Edgewood Junior High and Highland Park High School. "When we came home from school," adds Mrs. Souza, "we were expected to do our homework first and then we could play."

"HE CAME FROM A GENERATION THAT COULDN'T JUST FLIP A SWITCH; YOU HAD TO DO A LOT FOR YOURSELF."

Their father was organized and handy and liked to undertake home maintenance projects, if only to use his huge collection of hardware. "My dad thought that if one screwdriver is good, a set, or even two, is better," says John. "And there are so many different types of screws!" His father built a back porch on the house, and he and a friend installed a basketball goal on top of the garage for the kids. "The plans were so detailed, you'd think they were designing the Sears Tower," says John. "They fashioned the support structure out of two-and-a-half inch galvanized pipe. I believe that if a tornado had come along and blown the house to bits, the basketball goal would have remained intact."

"He liked to putter and figure out how things worked," explains Mrs. Souza. "He came from a generation that couldn't just flip a switch; you had to do for yourself." In summer Levine cut the grass, and in winter he shoveled snow from the gravel driveway.

He was not religious, says Mrs. Souza, but "considered himself traditional." Growing up, the family belonged to Jewish Reform congregations. The children received religious education on Sundays but "we weren't religious in the [deep] sense of the word. We observed certain traditions and holidays that were also part of the non-Jewish world." There was no talk of her father's experiences in the war, adds Maxine. The topic wasn't broached. "We didn't ask him about it—it wasn't part of the conversation."

John Levine remembers his father's personality as "cool," especially compared to the warmth exuded by his mother, adding, "And yet I always felt his love. He was away a lot; we didn't see as much of him as other kids would see their fathers. But when home he was always interested in us. He was not aloof by any means—he'd throw the ball in the backyard with me, and do things with us." Despite his hectic schedule, he faithfully attended the children's organ recitals and school assemblies and took them to ball games and movies.

For all that Levine cared about his business and military careers, his family was most important—his own and that of his relatives. He and Leah accepted nearly every family invitation to attend birthday parties, bar mitzvahs, and weddings. "Vacations were always family vacations," says John, usually trips to Minneapolis and Duluth, Minnesota (even in the dark of winter), to see uncles, aunts, and cousins. "When there was time for him to be a family man," says John, "he wanted to be a family man. He wanted to be with us. He also worked very hard so that my sister and me would have every advantage—would have things easier than they did." He let the kids know that they'd always get the support they needed.

Leah, meanwhile, maintained the house and looked after the kids. There was a lot to do. "Now that women work, housewives are sometimes looked at as having lives of leisure, but my mother was constantly busy, too," says John Levine. "Dad relied on my mother to take care of things around the house; if we needed a gardener or some other tradesman for a project, he suggested what we needed but left it to her to set things up and make things happen."

Leah, who at five feet, eight inches tall was nearly as tall as her husband, "was a warm, mild-mannered, giving person who always looked for the good in people," recalls John. "She could get along with anyone, no matter their income or social status." His sister agrees: "She was a wonderful listener—the best I've ever known. She was very generous with her time; she knew what to say and when to say it. People from all walks of life considered her their friend, mentor, confidante. She was unusual in that sense. She loved people."

More practically, she loved gardening and collecting antiques. She spent a lot of time in the garden and entered roses in local competitions, sometimes winning ribbons. She enjoyed browsing in local antique stores. And she liked to cook. "She cooked what my father liked," says Mrs. Souza, "and so we liked it, too. He was a simple eater. He was a meat loaf guy, with baked potatoes."

Leah Levine attended a lot of military social functions with her husband at nearby Fort Sheridan, where officers and their wives would eat dinner and, often, dance. The Levines liked to dance, as so many couples did in the 1950s, especially to songs by Frank Sinatra, Dean Martin, Bobby Darin, and Glenn Miller. Levine was a scotch drinker when socializing with civilian friends but stuck to wine (red, mostly) at military functions.

Fort Sheridan, named after the Civil War general Philip Sheridan, was established as a U.S. Army Post in the late 1880s, after the 1886 Haymarket labor riot in Chicago. The labor unrest (which involved demands for an eight-hour workday) spooked the business community. In 1887 the Commercial Club of Chicago, a group of prominent Chicago businessmen and politicians, purchased 600 acres along Lake Michigan, in Highwood, Illinois, and donated it to the federal government to house troops who could be called quickly to put down future insurrections. The fort's 227-foot high brick water tower—designed to resemble St. Mark's Campanile in Venice—became a landmark.

Not long after its construction, Major General Leonard Wood, Department of the East Commander between 1910 and 1914, conceived the idea of a reserve fighting force. He recognized the need "for training a standby force of men prepared for deployment in case of war," according to a history of Fort Sheridan, "and initiated the [idea] of reserve training camps independent of state and National Guard structure."

Fort Sheridan soon became the site of the first Reserve Officers Training Camp (ROTC), held in the summer of 1917 for 2,500 men. The fort was expanded dramatically to handle the thousands of new trainees and would eventually comprise more than one hundred buildings.

A second training camp immediately followed the first. "Approximately 5,800 men who had completed three months' basic training in the two successive camps were commissioned as officers in the Army Reserve," according to the fort's historical record, "applying in combat what they had learned in their training at Fort Sheridan. The type of training at the Fort reflected the situation in Europe at that time." Following the Declaration of War against Germany on April 6, 1917, additional Reserve Training Camps were created around the country. Fort Sheridan became an induction and Midwest training center for men entering the army from Illinois, Michigan, and Wisconsin.

The army effectively closed Fort Sheridan in the early 1990s and sold off most of the property for private development—only

"LEVINE WAS VERY DEVOTED TO THE ARMY RESERVE, AND FELT THAT HE COULD CONTRIBUTE A LOT."

a few military people are still stationed on a patch of the original site today—but it was still going strong in the 1950s and 1960s, when the Levines could be found there regularly. John Levine says that his mother didn't always have a lot in common with the active-duty wives at Fort Sheridan, but she befriended many of them and got involved with their activities at the base. "She, of her own initiative, got involved. I wouldn't say that any of the Fort Sheridan wives became close friends—but when there were social functions, whether large or small, she never felt that she was being dragged along to something. It was, yes, supporting my father, but also naturally who she was. And she never complained. Some might have said, 'Another one of these military functions'? But she looked forward to them." Adds Maxine Souza, "She supported his army activities 100 percent."

How could it be otherwise? Levine was "very devoted to the Army Reserve," Maxine explains, "and felt that he could contribute a lot. He took it very seriously. It was an important part of his life, and an important part of our lives." Though he was gone many weekends, and during the summer, Leah never perceived his absences as a family hardship—and so they weren't. As Maxine puts it, "She set the tone. And if you think about it, it's no different if someone's father goes off golfing every weekend." She recalls her father taking her and her brother with him to reserve summer encampments when they were in their teens. "They had special activities for the families—dinners, parades. It was fun."

IN THE EARLY 1960S, there came more promotions for the efficient, no-nonsense artillery officer. After five years as a lieutenant colonel, Levine was made a colonel in the fall of 1960 and then, in January 1962, appointed commanding officer of the XIV Corps Artillery, still based in Chicago. A little more than a year later, he was promoted to brigadier general—getting his first star. Levine said that a fellow brigadier general, also in artillery, pinned the silver star on each shoulder of his uniform.

The XIV Corps was active between 1942 and 1945 and again between 1957 and 1958. Its most notable achievements came in the Pacific theater in World War II, when under Major General Alexander Patch and, subsequently, Major General O.W. Griswold, it drove the Japanese from Guadalcanal and New Georgia in 1943, and in March 1944 defeated the formidable Japanese Seventeenth Army on Bougainville, which like Guadalcanal and New Georgia was part of the Solomon Islands chain. Thus the XIV Corps gained the nickname "Kings of the Solomons."

Brigadier General Levine, as commander of the XIV artillery, spent a lot of time at Fort McCoy, Wisconsin, especially for the annual two weeks of active-duty training. There are photos of him at Fort McCoy in July of 1963. One shows him, with visiting generals and officers, witnessing a demonstration by C Battery, Seventh Howitzer Division, of the fire power of a towed eight-inch howitzer and a self-propelled eight-inch howitzer. Another photo shows him, in his crisp olive drab uniform, giving instructions to a colonel about a field problem. Another shows Levine welcoming press people to the summer encampment. He is said to have done that frequently over the years to promote the army reserve.

Indeed, he must have played a role in getting Chicago mayor Richard J. Daley to proclaim an official "XIV Corps Artillery Day" every summer, for four or five years, in the early 1960s. Other photos show Brigadier General Levine inspecting the artillery Table of Organization and Equipment with a visiting general and trooping the line with various officers and dignitaries at the end-of-encampment artillery review.

That summer, Leah and the children visited their father at Fort McCoy—and John got an early lesson in leadership. Mom and the kids watched an artillery demonstration—all thumping retorts, noise, and smoke—and then all marched off to eat lunch with the reservists in the mess tent. "I'm eager to get in line for chow," recalls John. "I assume that since my dad is the commanding general, we'll get to go first. But dad holds us back. He later explained that 'a leader makes sure his men are fed before he eats.'"

As a military leader, Brigadier General Levine hewed to the military axiom that soldiers should move "up or out." He was demanding but fair—and always honest. He championed those officers under his command whom he felt were competent and professional—and encouraged their career development. Those who did not meet his standards were nudged out. John Levine says that his father felt it was his job "to protect the men from arbitrariness from above. He wanted to understand military objectives and what would be needed for his unit to succeed. His men, individually and as a unit, always knew that he had their interests at heart."

In 1966, following the inactivation of XIV Corps Artillery, Brigadier General Levine was given a new assignment. He was appointed Commanding General of the 416th Engineer Brigade. The brigade is still in existence, with its headquarters in Darien, Illinois. Brigadier General Levine had no engineering experience, but no matter: The army sent him to engineering school to learn. Engineering brigades are crucial to army military operations, of course. Their men are specialists in construction and destruction, geo-spatial mapping, land surveying, route clearance, and more. As the engineers put it, they build "up" (barracks, port facilities) and "out" (bridges, temporary airfields), sometimes in combat situations.

The basic mission, as outlined by the 416th Engineer Command itself, is to "facilitate the operational maneuver of decisive forces to destroy the enemy." In October 1990, the 416th was activated during Desert Shield and Desert Storm and took part in restoration and recovery operations in Kuwait. After a recent training exercise involving the construction of a moveable bridge across the Arkansas River, Lieutenant Colonel Jon Brierton, a battalion commander with the 416th, said, "There is all kinds of cool and sexy training here." That's surely not how Brigadier General Levine would have described his unit in the 1960s, which was involved in a lot of army reconstruction projects, but he is said to have been gratified to work with the brigade.

It was a brief stint. A year later, in March 1967, he was appointed Commanding General of the Eighty-fourth Division (Training), based in Milwaukee, with subordinate units scattered around Wisconsin. It was one of twelve training divisions in the USAR at that time. The primary purpose of a training division was (is) to visit regular army bases, typically during active duty, and "superimpose" its instructors on the operation—specifically the basic, advanced, and specialized training of new recruits. Training command officers would fall in behind the regular instructors at the base or even take over for them during the two-week tour. Some training divisions focus on armor, others specialize in signal corps or aviation. While an active-duty U.S. Army division might have 13,000 soldiers, reserve training units typically had roughly 3,000 troops.

The Eighty-fourth was a combat infantry division during both World War I and World War II. The division's history sup-posedly traces back to the Illinois militia to which Abraham Lincoln belonged during the 1832 Black Hawk War—hence its special designation as "The Railsplitters." In 2005 the division was renamed the Eighty-fourth Training Command, with its headquarters in Fort Knox, Kentucky.

In May 1967, barely three months into his new command, Levine was promoted to major general, earning a coveted second star. At that time, major general was the highest rank that an officer in the army reserve could achieve. (Now, the Chief of the Army Reserve is a three-star general.) Lieutenant General John H. Michaelis, a good friend, pinned the two sets of twin stars on Major General Levine in a ceremony. Michaelis, who was in the same class with General Douglas MacArthur at West Point, would later become commander of U.S. forces in Korea and a four-star general.

Major General Levine was no doubt thrilled by his new rank, but as those who knew him emphasize, he was a humble man not given to self-promotion or self-aggrandizement. Would he have been proud to have achieved that rank as a Jewish man, given that there were few Jews in the upper ranks of the military? Levine did not express such pride overtly to his family, according to his son, but then he was not a man who wore his religious identity like a war ribbon.

Says John Levine,

> On the one hand, I'd say, yes, it was a point of pride. You could be proud of something like that—'boy, I'm higher than any of my peers.' Or could it be just, 'Gee, I'm a Jew and look what I've accomplished in the United States.' I think he had a strong Jewish identity culturally—but I wouldn't see him as a religious person necessarily. There was internal pride, I'm sure. For somebody who achieved as much as he did, he was remarkably humble. He was the first to acknowledge that he was in the right place at the right time to achieve his promotions. He continued to do his job and the breaks came his way. I'd say there was pride—but maybe with a small 'p' as opposed to a capital 'p'.

LEVINE COMMANDED THE Eighty-fourth for two years before being reassigned to another infantry training division, the Eighty-fifth, in June 1969. That same year the army awarded him the Legion of Merit for his "superior performance in support of the Army Reserve program during the past ten years." He received the decoration at the Army Reserve Center in Milwaukee. He had earlier been the recipient of the Army Commendation Medal. "I hate to leave the 84th," said Major General Levine at his departure. "It is an outstanding reserve unit with unbelievable support from the people of Wisconsin. My two years here as commanding general have been the most rewarding of my career."

The Eighty-fifth would be equally so for him, and not just because it meant a convenient headquarters shift from Milwaukee back to his home city of Chicago. Part of the Fifth Army, the Eighty-fifth originally was a combat infantry division and known as the Custer Division, named after U.S. cavalry commander George Armstrong Custer. During World War I, one of its regiments fought alongside the White Army in the Russian Civil War. In World War II, the Eighty-fifth played a key role in the Italian campaign.

The Eighty-fifth had its headquarters on the north side of Chicago, at a building on the corner of Bryn Mawr and Kedzie avenues. About 150 people worked at the headquarters—a mix of officers and enlisted men: the commanding officer, chief of staff, and collection of G-staff personnel. The division comprised 2,700 soldiers, including a training command and four brigades, which had their own headquarters in different locations in Illinois. Each brigade, in turn, comprised four battalions, whose men were mostly the drill sergeants and instructors responsible for basic, active-duty training of new recruits, along with advanced training in marksmanship, communications, demolition, weapons, land navigation, and first aid. Under Major General Levine the division typically went to Fort Dix, Fort McCoy, or Fort Leonard Wood for its annual active-duty training. The division group would also go to Fort Ord for mobilization training—to familiarize itself with what it would be doing, with whom, and under what mission, were it to be mobilized.

The Eighty-fifth was a so-called Maneuver Training Command, organized to test various military units for their readiness

"INDIVIDUALS HAD TO DO THEIR JOBS PROPERLY AND WORK UNTIL THEY ACCOMPLISHED THEIR MISSION."

to deploy. "We would go to various units in the United States and check their records and see their training, evaluate their deployability and give them a rating," says former Major General (retired) Clifton Capp, who served as Levine's G1 for three years and later became assistant division commander. "If they needed work in certain areas, we'd tell them. We gave them deployment problems and would see if they could come up with solutions."

James Mukoyama, who served as a captain in the Eighty-fifth and who later become a major general and a training division commander himself, offered some insight into the responsibilities that Major General Levine would have faced. "Your function as a division commander is, first, to instill a sense of urgency and focus on the mission of the unit, which was to train soldiers for combat. Everything focused on that—to train soldiers to defend our nation. As division commander, your job was to make sure your unit understood the mission, was equipped to do the mission and could execute the mission." The ultimate goal, then, is to help trainees meet the standards needed to be successful.

Mukoyama says that Major General Levine "emphasized professionalism in the unit—that was very clear. By that I mean, he set a very high standard of performance. Individuals had to do their jobs properly and work until they accomplished their mission. We all knew what was expected. That's why we were successful— we had a very high degree of esprit and morale in the division."

Clifton Capp remembers Levine as "demanding" and a good leader. "He let you do your job, and if he didn't like it, he would tell you." He recalls Levine's first meeting after taking over the division. "There were several officers there who were in acting, or temporary, staff positions. He threw that out. He said, 'I don't go with this acting stuff—either you have a job or you don't, and I will determine that fairly soon.' He was a matter-of-fact type man. He expected nothing but excellence out of you or you were replaced. A lot of men left the 85th after he came on. They were either encouraged to leave by him, if they didn't do the job, or they were fearful of being asked to leave and left on their own."

Retired Major General James Bunting also served in the Eighty-fifth with Levine. Now living in Milwaukee, he was a G3, then later assistant division commander—and he, like Mukoyama, would go on to lead a division himself. "We were very compatible," he says of his relationship with Levine. "He was very decisive, and that made everyone's job easier, because they knew what to expect. In confidence, he could quickly resolve a situation." Good military leaders must be decisive, Bunting acknowledges, "but some people handle it better than others." He and others point out that in 1970, Major General Levine commissioned a redesign of the Eighty-fifth shoulder patch. It became a pentagon inside an octagon, and unit soldiers wore it for about ten years before another new design was created.

Levine's other good qualities, several people say, were his sense of fairness and his sense of empathy. "He always treated people equally and not condescendingly," says Mukoyama. "You always felt that he cared." In particular, he recognized that reservist duty entailed sacrifice by the men and their families. "We were a reserve unit, so we had to make sure that our soldiers and their families were taken care of. If a soldier is going through a divorce or going through problems at home, he or she is not going to be very effective in the unit. General Levine always emphasized family— that was an important lesson I learned from him personally."

Maxine Souza saw the same thing.

When we would go to an Army dinner with him, as the commander he would make the opening remarks. Invariably, he would thank my mother and say that without her support, he couldn't have made a career in the Reserve. Then he would thank the families of the men in his unit, every single time he spoke. It was a wonderful thing, and made me feel good because he wasn't there to glamorize himself. He was aware of the fact that being away from his family was made easier by the fact that my mother liked what he did and enjoyed his activities. It was beautiful to see that relationship.

Like every household, the Levine family suffered strains. "We did have our disagreements," says John. A significant one occurred when John graduated from high school, in 1969, and was preparing to attend the University of Michigan. America was in a febrile state in the late 1960s. Public sentiment against the Vietnam War was bubbling over, especially among young people. There were protests at numerous college campuses, including the University of Michigan, which was "radical" at the time, notes John.

How could there not be some friction between a socially and politically aware eighteen-year-old, who'd received a draft deferment, and the military officer who was his father? The major general wanted his son to join the ROTC in college and thus have a "leg up" should he end up in the military. John wasn't keen on the idea. "I wasn't anti-military but didn't want to serve if I didn't have to. I didn't want the conflict that would come with being associated with ROTC in that era." John says that his dad was "really disappointed" with his decision. "He thought I was wrong but was going to abide by the decision because it was mine."

As adults, the two later talked about the issue and essentially agreed to disagree. "He was listening to my side," says John, adding, "The dispute never really affected the quality of our relationship as adults. He was proud of me and what I was accomplishing, and it felt good that he was proud of me."

IN THE LATE 1960S AND EARLY 1970S Levine was busier than ever. In addition to his heavy military schedule, he was involved with a raft of civic organizations. At one time or another he was chairman of the Point of Purchase Advertising Institute, president of the Chicago Conference of Temple Mens' Clubs, and president of the Chicago Jewish Welfare Board Armed Service Council. Beyond that, he was president of the Fort Sheridan-Chicago

Chapter of the Association of the American Army and a member of the Reserve Officers Association. In 1973 he became a principal member of the Army Reserve Forces Policy Committee, which reviews all aspects of the reserve and makes recommendations to strengthen it.

Still, his command of the Eighty-fifth Training Division, with its nearly one hundred subordinate units spread around the state, dominated his time. He spent upwards of thirty weekends a year on military work, plus maybe four full weeks in the summer. It was a dedication that others noticed. He received a series of glowing reviews for his leadership of the Eighty-fifth. After an annual evaluation of the division and officer performance review, Major General Ward S. Ryan, who was with the Fifth Army at Fort Sheridan, wrote this in late 1971:

> Major General Levine's overall performance during his second year as commander of the 85th has been outstanding. He is astute, exceptionally well informed, and has taken positive action to improve overall readiness status of the division. He has developed an unusually high level of esprit de corps in his division. He is the best (most able) commander in the Northern Area of the Fifth U.S. Army.

Major General Chester L. Johnson, another rater that year, added that Major General Levine "has untiringly devoted all-out efforts toward improving the level of professionalism of the officers and NCOs (noncommissioned officers) of his unit. Attesting to his effectiveness, his unit performed in an outstanding manner during AT (Annual Training) '71; the unit conducted over 2,000 hours of instruction, of which only five hours were considered unsatisfactory."

A year later Major General Jack J. Wagstaff and Lieutenant General Patrick F. Cassidy evaluated Major General Levine's leadership. Wagstaff described him as "probably overall the best Reserve Component General Officer I have had the privilege of knowing in the year I have been on my present assignment; there are about 30 such officers in my jurisdiction." The evaluation noted that Levine and his wife "are charming and experienced participants in local military and civil social circles," and went on:

> General Levine is absolutely devoted to the Army and his country; intelligent, professional, hard and demanding. He takes particular pride in his program designed to educate his officers by frequent rotation; he relieves those who cannot maintain his standards. He can handle any position appropriate for his rank and should be used extensively, at least on a part-time basis, on the national level. He effectively implements that Army's Equal Opportunity Program; maintains a positive approach in all endeavors and imbues his staff and subordinate commanders with the same enthusiasm, loyalty and effectiveness typical of himself. His units consistently performed assigned tasks aggressively and exceeded minimum standards. Only 3 of 96 units failed to attain satisfactory AGI (annual general inspection) ratings or to maintain equipment effectively. MG Levine is an outstanding commander. His division reflects his leadership.

In a third evaluation, written in September and October 1973, Lieutenant General Patrick F. Cassidy, HQ Fifth Army, commanding general, and Lieutenant General Donn R. Pepke, HQ U.S. Army Forces Command, praised Major General Levine's performance in the "difficult and challenging environment facing contemporary reserve component commanders," especially his emphasis on the career development of his subordinates. The two added, "He is unusually productive in developing and pursuing new training techniques and is extremely innovative in his management of his unit during IDT (Inactive Duty Training), a difficult period for all reserve components. He has maintained a high overall readiness posture in the 85th Division and would provide the Army with a viable unit if mobilized. MG Levine is very clearly one of the most outstanding major generals serving in any component of the Army today."

IN THE SPRING OF 1975, William Levine's life changed dramatically—tragically. A few months earlier, Leah Levine had started complaining of a nagging cough. She'd been a lifelong smoker, so family members thought nothing of it. But the cough worsened, and in November 1974 she was diagnosed with lymphoma. She started receiving radiation and chemotherapy, but her condition quickly became grave.

At that time, Levine was preparing to leave for Fort Ord, California, where the Eighty-fifth Division would hold its annual training encampment. He was distraught about Leah's condition, but duty called. Leah surprised him by asking to go along. "She was in a bad way, but my mother wanted to go," recalls John. "She'd never been to that part of the country, and she wanted to be where he was." After all their time apart over the years, that would have been a strong desire at such a time. The two went off to California together. Not long after getting there, Leah Goldberg Levine suffered a stroke and died. She was sixty-one.

"It was horrible," says Maxine (Levine) Souza. "How do you cope with it? You don't expect it to happen. You hope for a better outcome, and it doesn't come. And then how do you put the pieces together?" She saw her father grieve as well. "That was almost harder than dealing with my own loss, because they were so devoted to each other. You knew he was devastated but did the best he could. In the last few years, when he would talk about her, he'd get that wispy tone in his voice and know that she was his one and only."

As that family tragedy unfolded, Levine retired from the army reserve. He'd turned sixty and, after a thirty-two-year career in the U.S. Army and USAR, spanning from May 1943 to July 1975, it was time to step away from the service work he so enjoyed. Hearing the news, several generals wrote to Levine, paying their respects. On July 19, 1975, two and half months after Leah's death, there was a formal Retirement Review ceremony (including Adjutant's Call, Inspection of Command, Ruffles and Flourishes, Posting of the Colors, and Pass in Review) for him at Fort Sheridan. Numerous family members and friends, including army officers with whom he'd served over the years, were in attendance.

Lieutenant General Allen J. Burdett presented Major General Levine with the Distinguished Service Medal Citation, given for "meritorious service to the Government of the United States in successive positions of great responsibility." He lauded Major General Levine's "outstanding personal example, professionalism and selfless dedication, which have contributed materially to the success of the Army Reserve Program." He added, "As a commander, General Levine has consistently demonstrated an early awareness of needed policy changes and has pioneered implementation of these proposals long prior to their being in effect Army-wide. His career-enhancing programs have resulted in significant improvements in the areas of morale and overall effectiveness of the individual reservist." Lieutenant General Burdett also noted Major General Levine's service on the Army Reserve Forces Policy Committee, which helped to "upgrade the Army Reserve as an overall entity."

And with that, Levine's military career ended on a gratifying but somber note. "The idea of serving his country had always been important to him," says John Levine.

That wasn't the last of the change that year. Levine also decided to resign from Lakeside Plastics. The firm had been rocked by change in recent years. Orrin Levine, William's brother, had died of a heart attack in 1966, at age forty-three. By then Lakeside Plastics was a public company that had branched out modestly into the sale of toys, in addition to selling advertising displays. In 1969 a company named Leisure Dynamics, a diversified toy company, bought Lakeside Plastics and changed its name to Lakeside Industries. By then the nature of the business had changed. Point-of-purchase clients were more interested in inexpensive signs than quality displays. Meanwhile, Leisure Dynamics was mostly interested in selling toys. "My dad objected to that," says John. "He thought they should devote more resources to the point-of-sale business. He was disgruntled about that."

Levine took his shares and resigned from Lakeside Industries. He started his own point-of-sale display business. It was similar to the old family firm but didn't enjoy the same success, and after a couple of years Levine got out of the business altogether. His life, as he'd known it for three decades, was over. Suddenly, Levine was adrift. His two jobs were gone—and so, worst of all, was his wife of more than thirty years. How could he cope?

He didn't. He stopped eating, lost weight, slept fitfully, and fell into a depressed and frazzled state of mind that stretched out over two years. Weak and frail, he couldn't write and could barely walk. He was hospitalized, diagnosed with Parkinson's disease, and put on medication. Levine later told an interviewer that he'd had a nervous breakdown, adding, "I could cope with everyone's problems but my own."

Relief came in the form of another companion—Rhoda Kreiter. Like Levine, she'd been happily married but lost her spouse in 1975, also to cancer, the same week in May when Leah Levine died. The two had never met but lived a stone's throw from one another in Highland Park. A mutual friend suggested that William and Rhoda get together. He called her, and they agreed to have dinner. "I thought he was quiet and he looked sad," recalls Rhoda. "I felt sorry for him." The two spent most of the evening talking about their former spouses and good first marriages. Rhoda had been married to David Kreiter, a journalist-turned-owner of a graphics supply company. "It was good that we could do that. That's how we started."

The two got along, and in 1977 found themselves dating. They continued to see each other, and after about two years Rhoda, who is petite and perky and knows her own mind, could sense a coming proposal. "I was a little nervous about it," she remembers. "How good could another marriage be after the one I just had?'

I told him, 'Don't ask me to marry you—I'm not ready—but don't ask anyone else. I'm interested, but not now."

Early on in their relationship, Levine told Rhoda that doctors thought he had Parkinson's disease. This puzzled Rhoda, who responded, "Well, do you or don't you"? She'd seen him walk, watched his hands, and didn't see the symptoms of the disease. Levine went to the Great Lakes Naval Hospital for another checkup, and the doctors there started reducing his medication level. He responded well. Rhoda then persuaded him to see a neurologist. In the end, doctors determined that he did not have Parkinson's. "I was quite normal then and didn't even know it," Levine said later. "That was funny."

After three years together, and then a brief separation, Levine gave Rhoda an ultimatum of sorts: "Either we get married or I'm going to walk." Rhoda agreed to marry him. Levine took Rhoda to Minnesota to meet both his family and Leah's, including her sisters. He, in turn, met and spent time with both sides of Rhoda's family—her three daughters (Robin Plotkin, Shelley Solow, and Susan Margolis), their husbands, and the family of Rhoda's late husband. "He was so gracious," says John. "That open acceptance endeared him to people."

William and Rhoda exchanged vows and rings in 1980, at a small ceremony at the Am Shalom synagogue in Glencoe, Illinois. "It was a very smart thing for the both of us," says Rhoda. "We had 33 happy years." Levine, during an interview years later, said, "I never thought I'd have another chance [at love]; in fact I was resigned to it." Their marriage, he said, was "wonderful."

Levine sold his house and two acres of property on Green Bay Road and moved into Rhoda's house on nearby South Deere Park

Drive. (Three new houses were built on the Green Bay parcels, one by one of Rhoda's daughters.) Rhoda and her first husband had built the Deere Park house, and she'd lived there since 1957. "I joke that he married me because of my large basement," says Rhoda. "He couldn't use his own garage because it was full of so much stuff. He was such a pack rat; he saved everything."

"HE JUST PICKED UP THE CARDS AND PLAYED. HE NEVER REALLY LEARNED THE RULES."

The new couple stayed busy. Levine was involved for many years with the Reserve Officers' Association (ROA), an organization supporting reservists and their role in national defense; the Association of the United States Army (AUSA), which fosters communication and cooperation between army reservists and the corporate sphere; and local area military retiree organizations, including branches at Fort McCoy and Fort Sheridan. He attended annual ROA, AUSA, and commander conferences in Washington for many years after his retirement. He continued to do volunteer work for the Ravinia Festival, and he and Rhoda were avid bridge players. Levine was said to be a crackerjack player with an unusual style. He never sorted his hand and made peculiar bids, says Merril Levine, John's wife. "He just picked up his cards and played. He never really learned the rules." The two took a class on comparative religions.

In addition, Rhoda volunteered for many years with Chicago Action for Soviet Jewry, a local branch of the Union of Councils of Soviet Jewry. The group's aim was to help Jewish people in the former Soviet republics, in any way it could. It did its own fundraising and mailed clothes, medical equipment (wheelchairs, crutches, walkers), and money to needy families. Sixty-five U.S. synagogues were matched with cities in the Baltic, Siberia, and southern Eurasian republics, and they helped Jews in those areas establish Hebrew schools and "learn how to practice Judaism," says Rhoda, "because they'd been denied the education that would have taught them." Rhoda also helped American kids of bar mitzvah and bat mitzvah age to befriend young Jews in the former Russian republics, and she went to Washington to help lobby to maintain the then immigration quota of 40,000 annually for Soviet Jews. William pitched in as well, going to the office to help pack boxes of supplies for mailing.

One year the couple took a trip with other members of Chicago Action for Soviet Jewry to three cities in Russia and three cities in Ukraine, bringing with them money and religious books for the families they would meet. Rhoda remembers a rough three-hour ride from Moscow to Tula. There were no gas stations (the driver carried cans of extra gas in his car) and no bathrooms. They stayed with a family that had no plumbing, met a few other Jewish families in Tula, and went to a meeting hall that served as their synagogue.

Levine spent a lot of time with Rhoda's daughters and their children. Jonathan Plotkin, Robin's husband, was particularly fond of Levine. He recalls meeting the general in 1980, two weeks after Levine's marriage to Rhoda. After finishing graduate school in Boston, Plotkin decided to take a break and hitchhike across the country. He aimed to spend a week in California. On the way he got a driver to drop him off on the outskirts of Chicago. Plotkin was old friends with Rhoda's family and had known Robin since the two were little kids. He planned to grab a meal and a shower at Rhoda's. Plotkin's phone call to Rhoda was answered by her new husband, who, when he learned of Jonathan's longtime friendship with Rhoda, insisted that he come to the house. "He ordered me to do it," recalls Plotkin, who complied. He and the Levines and one or two of Rhoda's others daughters went out for dinner. Robin showed up, too—"and that night she decided, then and there, that we were going to get married."

They did, and the couple eventually had four children. The family became very close to William Levine. "For thirty-five years he was my mentor, confidante, grandfather to my kids—involved in every aspect of their lives," says Plotkin. "People told me he was a tough guy, fair and reasonable but tough. We only knew him as the most loving and giving person imaginable."

THERE IS LITTLE IN LEVINE'S military record, nor any personal effects, confirming his presence at Dachau. There is only his memory—and that, he says, he did not tamper with until the spring of 1983, when he spoke about Dachau for the first time since the war. In a 1997 interview with the University of Southern California Shoah Foundation, established by filmmaker Steven Spielberg to record Holocaust testimonies, Levine recalls being asked that year to give a talk to students at Evanston High School about his experiences during World War II. He talked about Dachau and the Holocaust but broke down and could not continue.

But after speaking to the students, Levine was hit by a

startling realization—that keeping his Dachau experience a secret for so long was "wrong, quite wrong." From that point forward he became a public speaker.

LEVINE GAVE SPEECHES sporadically in the following years. ahead. He spoke at synagogues and at parlor gatherings in the Chicago suburbs; he talked to students at DePaul University and gave testimony at the Illinois Holocaust Museum and Education Center, which has one of his general officer sidearms (a Colt 911) in a permanent display.

"OUR JOB IS TO MEET THE CHALLENGE AND MAKE OUR STRATEGY OF DETERRENCE WORK."

His talks focused, naturally, on World War II, Dachau, and the need for America to be strong and vigilant. In a 1969 Memorial Day speech at the Sholom Memorial Park in Palatine, Illinois, at the height of the Vietnam War, Levine decried antiwar cynics, saying, "It is now somewhat unfashionable to speak of patriotism and idealism, to fly the flag, to proclaim in depth what America stands for and what our freedom cost us. Nevertheless, we know the meaning of all these, and it is precisely this knowledge that has motivated our soldiers and allowed the heat of a thousand battles to temper America, not consume her." He went on, "Certainly modern war is appalling. But the idea that there is nothing worse—that our only objective is survival—is outright defeatism...

Our whole history proves beyond any question that apathy and defeatism has no application to the American character."

He echoed that idea in 1985, when Ronald Reagan was president. Speaking to a North Shore Jewish men's group, he reviewed the Soviet Union's strategic missile threat and emphasized the need for the United States to strengthen its own ballistic and conventional forces, saying, "Our job is to meet the challenge and make our strategy of deterrence work."

IN THE LATE 1980S AND 1990S Levine put his service ethic to work on behalf of local synagogues that were building new facilities. In 1989 the Moriah Congregation in Deerfield, Illinois, decided to completely expand its building. William and Rhoda were members of the Moriah Congregation, and William, having led an engineering brigade, offered to be the owner's representative on the project—the person authorized to sign or modify contracts on behalf of the client and ensure that the general contractor completes the work on time and on budget.

Every morning, Levine got up early, put on a hard hat, and went to the Moriah job site, where he'd keep an eye on things, ask questions, and interact with the workers. "The general knew the name of every man who worked on his job site, from the master carpenter to the journeyman plumber," says Phillip Kupritz, an architect and principal at K2 Studio in Chicago, who designed the Moriah project and two other North Shore buildings on which Levine was the owner's representative. "He got to know his troops, so to speak."

Kupritz says that while the general was not an expert on commercial construction, he could read blueprints, understand drawings. "He was a process-oriented person, which is to say that he asked the right questions and expected the right answers."

Levine, Kupritz, and general contractor Nate Pinkus, among others, would have weekly meetings to review the progress of construction, discuss problems, and talk about the work schedule for the week ahead. The day before the meeting, Levine would get everyone on the phone to make sure they were all prepared for the meeting. "If you had to get something done," says Kupritz, "he made sure you were on your toes and didn't wait until the last minute. If there were calls that needed to be made—a subcontractor who didn't have his drawings done on time or one of a thousand other things, he'd make the calls." While Pinkus generally ran the meetings, all issues would be run past the general.

"He led from up front," says Kupritz. "He had that command of what needed to be done and how to get it done, and he didn't flinch if something was missed. He understood human nature and knew people weren't perfect. If something required an increase in project cost, he would defend it and make it happen." When workers left the job site at the end of a day, the place had to be clean and well organized, with tools and equipment put away properly, all ready for the next day.

After the Moriah project was completed, Levine worked as the owner's representative on a major renovation of the B'nai Tikvah Congregation in Deerfield, Illinois, completed in 1992, and on the construction of a new Sager Solomon Schecter Day School for elementary and middle-school students in Northbrook, completed in 1994. He took no money for any of the work. "He did it because he wanted to help the various organizations with which he was involved become stronger," says Kupritz. Adds Mrs. Levine, "He said that he wouldn't enjoy it as much if he were getting paid."

Levine also got involved in a morning prayer service at Moriah Congregation, called a Morning Minyon. He'd come in early and make coffee, put out sweet rolls and lox, so that the ten or fifteen people who came to the service every day—mostly men—would have something to eat. As he had in the army, Levine always tasted the coffee first, to make sure that it was hot. "He liked to say, 'the coffee is 'ot," dropping the "h," "let's get going," says Kupritz. "It was a little funny thing. If someone arrived and said to the general, 'It's good to see you,' he'd respond: 'It's good to be seen.' He had a sense of humor. I had a picture of how a major general might behave, and he messed it up."

In 2001, when he was eighty-five, Levine and Plotkin attended a Holocaust Memorial weekend in Washington, D.C. Survivors were honored along with the liberators of the concentration camps. At a formal dinner, Levine sat with a few survivors. According to Plotkin, "One looked at him and said, 'You are a hero.' William started to cry and said, 'I'm not a hero—I'm not a hero.' I could tell by the way he was weeping that something deep was imbedded in him."

Levine, to his credit, did not like being called a hero or characterized as "the liberator of Dachau." Said he, "I don't like that term—I've always been uncomfortable with it. It implies that I liberated the camp. I didn't. Goodness knows, there were many people involved in the liberation process. If I'm classified as one of the many who liberated the camp, I'd feel more comfortable."

In 2005, when he turned ninety, Levine received various tributes. One came in the form of a note from President George

W. Bush, who thanked Levine for his "60 years of service to the Army, Army Reserve, retiree affairs organizations and the nation." Lieutenant General James R. Helmly, Chief of the Army Reserve, wrote him as well, stating, "Please know that your efforts and hard work on behalf of the Army Reserve have been deeply appreciated."

His extended family also showed their respect. "You've added such an incredible dimension to our family," wrote Robin Plotkin. "Your love, care and concern for us all is so appreciated." David Solow, son of Rhoda's daughter Shelley Solow, wrote Levine, addressing him as "Pa," and said, "I find it exceedingly difficult to praise you in a manner befitting the enormous impact you've had on my family and my life. I constantly marvel at your never ending supply of wisdom, your great sense of humor and heartfelt love for all of us. I only hope that I age half as gracefully as you have."

That same year Levine drove to Paducah, Kentucky, for the last reunion of the Thirty-fourth AAA group, his World War II unit. Of twenty or so surviving members that year, six were in attendance. Levine had attended nearly all of the unit's reunions since 1973. A few years later, the major general made his last appearance in a dress uniform, at a U.S. Holocaust Museum luncheon in Chicago—an annual fundraiser that attracts some 2,500 people. He marched into the room with other military personnel, some carrying flags representing the various concentration camps.

By then Levine had fulfilled what he considered his final mission: telling people about war and about hatred and about Dachau, so they could work to ensure that it doesn't happen again. "The world cannot survive another event such as the Holocaust," Levine said in one interview. "It can't. We will lose all our humanity."[15]

Education was crucial, but he wasn't certain that it could stop the problem of parents passing down prejudicial attitudes to their young children. "There must be some way for a parent to raise a child in formative years, from age one to five, without any kind of prejudice—color prejudice, [religious] prejudice, gender prejudice, any kind. That is the key; if we find that key, we'll have no more racial problems, no more genocide."

In 2013, ninety-seven-year-old Major General William Percival Levine passed away at his Highland Park home in the North Shore of Chicago where he lived for more than sixty years. He had never forgotten the joys or the horrors of being a citizen soldier during World War II, the faces of death or the looks of gratitude. He had recognized and fulfilled what he considered a responsibility to serve—his family, his Jewish community, and his country.

There are two tributes to his life at the Moriah Congregation, Deerfield, Illinois. Inside the building there is a plaque, written by then Rabbi Samuel Fraint, that calls Levine the "foundation rock" of the synagogue. Fraint lauds Levine's "spirit, his optimism, his sense of humor, his wisdom and intelligence, and above all the genuine care and concern he had for every single person. A sweet, smart, salty, sage man, he was proud to be an American and proud to be a Jew. He was loved and respected here." Outside, there is the William P. Levine Circle—a charming little garden with hedge bushes and pear trees. Levine's red, two-star general's flag flutters on a pole in the center of the circle, above a second plaque attached to a large rock. It reads, "For service above and beyond the call of duty. And the coffee is always 'ot."

Endnotes

1   United States Holocaust Memorial Museum interview
    with William P. Levine, May 23, 1990.

2   Interview with William P. Levine, May 23, 1990.

3   Interview with William P. Levine, May 23, 1990.

4   Orah Arif, "It Was Too Terrible for Me to Want to Remember,"
    William P. Levine papers, Pritzker Museum & Military Library.

5   http://articles.chicagotribune.com/2013-04-22/news/ct-met-general-levine-
    obit-20130422_1_levine-dachau-concentration-camp.

6   Interview with William P. Levine, May 23, 1990.

7   Arif, "It Was Too Terrible for Me to Want to Remember."

8   Interview with William P. Levine, May 23, 1990.

9   Arif, "It Was Too Terrible for Me to Want to Remember."

10 Arif, "It Was Too Terrible for Me to Want to Remember."

11 Jewish Chronicle, November 29, 1985.

12 Testimony of Leon Kotlowsky, in "Jews in Wartime 1939–45," by Jack Lennard,
    Levine collection, Pritzker Military Museum & Library.

13 Testimony of Leon Kotlowsky.

14 Chicago Tribune, undated press cutting, William P. Levine archives,
    Pritzker Military Museum & Library.

15 Chicago Tribune, undated press cutting, William P. Levine archives,
    Pritzker Military Museum & Library.

Selected Bibliography

Part One

Abzug, Robert. *Inside the Vicious Heart*. New York: Oxford University Press, 1985.

Adler, Laure. *Marguerite Duras, A Life*. Chicago: University of Chicago Press, 2000.

Antelme, Robert. *The Human Race*. Evanston, IL: The Marlboro Press, 1998.

Arnold-Foster, Mark. *The World at War*. New York: Stein & Day, 1973.

Bessel, Richard. *Germany 1945*. New York: Harper Collins, 2009.

Bishop, Leo V., George A. Fisher, and Frank J. Glasglow. *The Fighting Forty-Fifth: The Combat Report of an Infantry Division*. Baton Rouge, LA: Army & Navy Publishing Co., 1946.

Brome, Vincent. *The Way Back*. New York: W.W. Norton & Company, 1957.

Brooks, Barbara. *With Utmost Spirit*. Lexington, KY: University of Kentucky Press, 2004

Buechner, Emajean. *Sparks: The Combat Diary of a Battalion Commander*. Metarie, LA: Thunderbird Press, 1991.

Buechner, Howard A. *Dachau: Hour of the Avenger*. Metarie, LA: Thunderbird Press, 1986.

Cundiff, Paul A. *45th Division CP: A Personal Record from World War II*. Privately published. Place and date unknown.

Dachau and Nazi Terror, 1933-1945, Studies and Reports II, Dachau, 2002.

Dann, Sam. *Dachau, 29 April 1945*. Lubbock, TX: Texas Tech University Press, 1998.

Die Letzen Tage von Nurnberg. Nuremberg: Edited 8 Uhr Blatt, 1952.

Distel, Barbara. "The Liberation of the Concentration Camp Dachau." Dachauer Hefte 1. Verlag Dachauer Hefte. Dachau, 1985.

Duras, Marguerite. *The War*. New York: The New Press, 1985.

Eisenhower, D. *Crusade in Europe*. New York: Doubleday, 1948.

Letters to Mamie. New York: Doubleday, 1978.

Ellis, John. *The Sharp End, the Fighting Man in WWII*, New York: Charles Scribner's Sons, 1980.

Embry, John. *The 45th Infantry Division at Anzio* (Monograph No. 8). Oklahoma City, OK: 45th Infantry Division Museum, 1986.

Evans, Richard J. *The Third Reich at War*. New York: Penguin, 2009.

Fritz, Stephen. *Endkampf*. Lexington, KY: University of Kentucky Press, 2004.

Fussell, Paul. *Wartime*. New York: Oxford University Press, 1989.

Gun, Nerin. *The Day of the Americans*. New York: Fleet Publishing, 1966.

Hallowell, Jack, et al. *Eager for Duty. History of the 157th Infantry Regiment* (Rifle). Oklahoma City: Privately published, 1946.

Hitchcock, William I. *The Bitter Road to Freedom*. New York: Free Press, 2008.

Israel, David. *The Day the Thunderbird Cried*. Medford, OR: Emek Press, 2005.

Judt, Tony. *Europe*. New York: Penguin, 2005.

Keegan, John. *The Second World War*. New York: Penguin, 1989.

Kern, Erich. *Verbrechen am deutschen Volk, Eine Dokumentation alliierter Grausamkeiten*. Gottingen, 1964.

Kershaw, Ian. *Hitler 1936-1945, Nemesis*. New York: W.W. Norton, 2000.

Merridale, Catherine. *Ivan's War*. New York: Henry Holt, 2006.

Moorehead, Alan. *Eclipse*. New York: Harper, 1968.

Nelson, Guy. *Thunderbird: A History of the 45th Infantry Division*. Oklahoma City, OK: 45th Infantry Division Association, 1970.

Patch, Alexander. "The Seventh Army: From the Vosges to the Alps." *Army and Navy Journal*, December, 1945.

Perry, Michael W. *Dachau Liberated*. Seattle: Inkling Books, 2000.

Pyle, Ernie. *Brave Men*. New York: Henry Holt, 1944.

Rawson, Andrew. *In Pursuit of Hitler*. Barnsley, UK: Pen and Sword, 2008.

Reynolds, Quentin. *The Curtain Rises*. New York: Random House, 1944.

Rothchild, Sylvia. *Voices from the Holocaust*. New York: New American Library, 1981.

Sevareid, Eric. *Not So Wild a Dream*. New York: Knopf, 1946.

Smith, Marcus J. *The Harrowing of Hell: Dachau*. Albuquerque: University of New Mexico Press, 1972.

Terkel, Studs. *The Good War*. London: Hamish Hamilton, 1985.

Toland, John. *The Last 100 Days*. New York: Random House, 1966.

Trevor-Roper, Hugh. *The Last Days of Hitler*. New York: Macmillan, 1965.

Part Two

The official United States military record of Major General William Levine.

The papers of William Levine, housed at the Pritzker Military Museum & Library archive, Chicago, Illinois.

United States Holocaust Memorial Museum, interview with William P. Levine, May 23, 1990.

Interviews with Rhoda Levine, second wife of General William Levine, March-April 2016

Interviews with John Levine, son of General William Levine, March-April 2016.

Interview with Merril Levine, wife of John Levine, April 2016.

Interview with Maxine (Levine) Souza, daughter of General William Levine, March 2016.

Interviews with Major General (retired) James Mukoyama, March-April 2016.

"The Long Watch," March-April 1953 issue of *W.E. Journal, (Western Electric Co., Inc.),* Reprinted in the July-August 1953 issue of *Antiaircraft Journal.*

Encyclopedia of Chicago: "History of Highland Park, Illinois" (http://www. encyclopedia.chicagohistory.org/pages/580.html).

Highland Park, Illinois Historical Society (http://highlandparkhistory.com/).

Encyclopedia of Chicago: "Fort Sheridan, Illinois" (http://www.encyclopedia. chicagohistory.org/pages/478.html).

Fort Sheridan.org.

416th Engineer Command, official website (https://www.army.mil/416thtec).

Lieutenant Colonel Jon Brierton, battalion commander with the 416th Engineer Command (https://www.army.mil/416thtec).

Interview with Major General (retired) Clifton Capp, May 2016.

Interview with Major General (retired) James Bunting, May 2016.

United States Army Reserve 84th Division (Training) website (http://www.usar.army.mil/Commands/Training/84th-TN).

Comment by Major General Ward S. Ryan from 1971 military performance review of Major General Levine, Pritzker Military Museum & Library archives.

Comment by Major General Chester L. Johnson from 1972 military performance review of Major General Levine, Pritzker Military Museum & Library archives.

Comments by Major General Jack J. Wagstaff and Lieutenant General Patrick F. Cassidy from performance review of Major General William Levine, Pritzker Military Museum & Library archives.

Comments by Lieutenant General Donn R. Pepke, HQ U.S. Army Forces Command, and Lieutenant General Patrick F. Cassidy, HQ Fifth Army, commanding general, from a September-October 1973 performance review of Major General Levine's units, Pritzker Military Museum & Library archives.

Comments of Lieutenant General Allen M. Burdett, Jr., upon awarding Major General Levine the Distinguished Service Medal 1997, papers of William Levine, Pritzker Military Museum & Library archives.

University of Southern California Shoah Foundation interview of General Levine August 7, 1997, https://www.youtube.com/watch?v=IPr9r4jh8rc; https://sfi.usc.edu/.

Interview with Jonathan Plotkin, friend of William Levine, March 2016.

Interview with Phillip Kupritz, architect at K2 Studio, Chicago, April 2016.

Letter to William Levine from Robin Plotkin, daughter of Rhoda (Kreiter) Levine, Papers of William Levine, Pritzker Military Museum & Library archives.

Letter to William Levine from David Solow, son of Rhoda Levine's daughter Shelley Solow, Papers of William Levine, Pritzker Military Museum & Library archives.

Dedication plaque for William Levine from Moriah Congregation and then-Rabbi Samuel Friant, Deerfield, Illinois.

About the Authors

Alex Kershaw is a *New York Times* best-selling author of *The Liberator* and several other widely acclaimed books about World War II.

Richard Ernsberger, Jr. is a longtime magazine writer who served as an editor and reporter at *Newsweek* for over 20 years, and at *American History* and *World War II*.

Acknowledgments

"The General" Team
Colonel (IL) Jennifer N. Pritzker, IL ARNG (Retired): Executive Editor
Kenneth Clarke: Executive Editor, Creative Director
Wendy Palitz: Designer, Creative Director
Michael W. Robbins: Contributing Editor
Jennifer Berry: Photo Researcher
Sharon Brinkman: Copy Editor
Stephen Callahan: Indexer
Andrew Pritzker: PMML Research Intern
Dr. Waitman Beorn: PMML Scholar in Residence 2013-2014

Special Thanks
Major General William P. Levine (1915-2013)
Rhoda Levine, John Levine and the entire Levine family
Mark D. Wasserman

Pritzker Military Museum & Library Board of Directors
Colonel (IL) J. N. Pritzker, IL ARNG (Retired), Founder and Chair
Tyrone C. Fahner

Lieutenant Commander Arie Friedman, MD, USNR-R (MC) (Retired)
Major General James Mukoyama, U.S. Army (Retired)
Scott Murray
Master Sergeant Ginny Narsete, USAF (Retired)
John W. Rowe
Robert E. Sarazen
John H. Schwan
Captain John A. Williams, PhD, USNR (Retired)
Kenneth Clarke, Ex-Officio

Pritzker Military Museum & Library Staff
Kenneth Clarke, President and CEO
Teri Embrey, Chief Librarian
Kat Latham, Director of Collection Management
Megan Williams, Director of External Affairs
Martin Billheimer, Library Clerk
Olivia Button, Digital Collections Coordinator
Dustin DePue, Special Collections Librarian
Paul W. Grasmehr, Reference Coordinator
Brad Guidera, Production Manager
Rachel Kosmal, Marketing and Communications Coordinator
Tina Louise Happ, Associate Chief Librarian
John LaPine, Collection Services Manager
Lee May, Development and Membership Coordinator
Susan Mennenga, WWI Centennial Project Manager
Chris Meter, Administrative Assistant
Aaron Pylinski, Production Coordinator
Katie Strandquist, Special Events Manager
Lindsey Sturch, Librarian
Thomas Webb, Oral History Coordinator

Index

MAJ. GEN. R.T. FREDERICK
COMMANDING

LT. GEN. A.M. PATCH
COMMANDING

AA OFFICER
BRIG. GEN. P.B. KELLY

UNITS PARTICIPATING

23d AAA GROUP
COL. J.B. FRASER
COMMANDING

34th AAA GROUP
COL. P.A. ROY
COMMANDING

62d AAA GUN BN
LT. COL. A.S. BUYNOSKI
COMMANDING

214th AAA GUN BN
LT. COL. C.W. KEITZMAN
COMMANDING

106th AAA AW BN (M)
LT. COL. H.H. ARNOLD
COMMANDING

436th AAA AW BN (M)
LT. COL. A.H. SCHUTZ
COMMANDING

441st AAA AW BN (SP)
LT. COL. T.H. LEARY
COMMANDING

569th AAA AW BN (M)
LT. COL. E.W. SHERMAN
COMMANDING

777th AAA AW BN (SP)
LT. COL. H. TWYMAN JR.
COMMANDING

798th AAA AW BN (M)
LT. COL. F.W. LEDEBOER
COMMANDING

838th AAA AW BN (M)
LT. COL. D.B. WEBBER
COMMANDING

895th AAA AW BN (M)
LT. COL. Y.W. WOLFE
COMMANDING

910th AAA AW BN (M)
LT. COL. E.H. SHUMATE
COMMANDING

353d AA SLT BN
LT. COL. J.A. COURTENAY
COMMANDING

572d AAA AW BN (SP)
LT. COL. L.W. HATTOX
COMMANDING

MAJ. GEN. R.R. ALLEN
COMMANDING

OSTHOFEN
ABENHEIM
NORDHEIM
BEISELHEIM
PFEDDERSHEIM
WORMS
HORCHHEIM
WIES-OPPENHEIM

RHINE
ALTRHEIN
TREADWAY BRIDGE
HEAVY PONTON BRIDGE
HEAVY PONTON

LEGEND
- 40 MM.
o 50 CAL.
90 MM.
SEARCHLIGHT
OBSERVATION POST
BRIDGE